QUESTIONS AND ANALYSIS IN HISTORY

Edited by Stephen J. Lee, Sean Lang and Jocelyn Hunt

Other titles in the series:

Modern History

Imperial Germany, 1871–1918
Stephen J. Lee

The Weimar Republic
Stephen J. Lee

Hitler and Nazi Germany
Stephen J. Lee

The Spanish Civil War
Andrew Forrest

The Cold War
Bradley Lightbody

Stalin and the Soviet Union
Stephen J. Lee

Parliamentary Reform, 1785–1928
Sean Lang

British Foreign and Imperial Policy, 1865–1919
Graham D. Goodlad

The French Revolution
Jocelyn Hunt

The First World War
Ian C. Cawood and David McKinnon-Bell

Early Modern History

The English Wars and Republic, 1636–1660
Graham E. Seel

The Renaissance
Jocelyn Hunt

Tudor Government
T.A. Morris

Spain, 1474–1598
Jocelyn Hunt

The Early Stuart Kings, 1603–1642
Graham E. Seel and David L. Smith

ANGLO-IRISH RELATIONS, 1798–1922

NICK PELLING

ROUTLEDGE

London and New York

First published 2003
by Routledge
11 New Fetter Lane, London EC4P 4EE

Simultaneously published in the USA and Canada
by Routledge
29 West 35th Street, New York, NY 10001

Routledge is an imprint of the Taylor & Francis Group

Typeset in Grotesque MT, Scala Sans and Perpetua by
BC Typesetting, Bristol
Printed and bound in Great Britain by
TJ International Ltd, Padstow, Cornwall

British Library Cataloguing in Publication Data
A catalogue record for this book is available from the British Library

Library of Congress Cataloging in Publication Data
Pelling, Nick.
Anglo-Irish relations, 1798–1922/Nick Pelling.
    p.   cm. – (Questions and analysis in history)
Includes bibliographical references and index.
ISBN 0–415–28671–9 (alk. paper) – ISBN 0–415–24039–5 (pbk.: alk. paper)
1. Ireland–Foreign relations–Great Britain.   2. Great Britain–
Foreign relations–Ireland.   3. Ireland–Relations–England.
4. England–Relations–Ireland.   I. Title. II. Series.

DA47.9.I75 P45 2002
327.415041–dc21
    2002009319

ISBN 0–415–28671–9 (hbk)
ISBN 0–415–24039–5 (pbk)

To my wife, Helen, who is more Irish than me

CONTENTS

SERIES PREFACE

Most history textbooks now aim to provide the student with interpretation, and many also cover the historiography of a topic. Some include a selection of sources.

So far, however, there have been few attempts to combine *all* the skills needed by the history student. Interpretation is usually found within an overall narrative framework and it is often difficult to separate the two for essay purposes. Where sources are included, there is rarely any guidance as to how to answer the questions on them.

The Questions and Analysis series is therefore based on the belief that another approach should be added to those which already exist. It has two main aims.

The first is to separate narrative from interpretation so that the latter is no longer diluted by the former. Most chapters start with a background narrative section containing essential information. This material is then used in a section focusing on analysis through a specific question. The main purpose of this is to help you tighten up essay technique.

The second aim is to provide a comprehensive range of sources for each of the issues covered. The questions are of the type which appear on examination papers, and some have worked answers to demonstrate the techniques required.

The chapters may be approached in different ways. The background narratives can be read first to provide an overall perspective, followed by the analyses and then the sources. The alternative method is to work through all the components of each chapter before going on to the next.

INTRODUCTION

It was the British Prime Minister David Lloyd George who came closest to summing up imperial frustration with Ireland when he likened discussions with the Irish leader Eamon de Valera to 'picking up mercury with a fork'. De Valera's amusingly unhelpful response, that he should 'use a spoon',[1] perfectly captures the spirit of mutual, and no doubt wilful, incomprehension that has bedevilled modern Anglo-Irish relations.

But the history of Anglo-Irish relations is perhaps even more slippery than Lloyd George had thought. What particularly makes the history so difficult is the fact that far too many historians have used the writing of history as a means of perpetuating the conflict they purport to delineate. For Irish nationalists reflecting on what might be seen as several centuries of colonial oppression, the writing of history has been the one arena in which old wrongs and injustices could be highlighted and, to some extent, righted. Hence in the mid-nineteenth century the Young Ireland and Fenian movements devoted great energy to creating a nationalist version of Anglo-Irish history. That tradition has continued, though in rather more subtle terms, down to the present day.

On the British, or, to be more apt, *English* side of the historiographical divide there has been less of a sustained tradition and more of a set of racist assumptions, most of which can be traced back to imperialist historians, such as Froude, in the nineteenth century. Indeed it is tempting to believe that the English 'Irish joke' is the distilled left-over of Victorian imperialist historiography. Even today many English students tend to revert to such approaches once the subject reveals its more mercurial side.

But perhaps the most interesting response to this abuse of the past emerged in Ireland in the late 1960s and 1970s. Irish historians such as F.S.L. Lyons began to subject nationalist myth to rigorous historical analysis and as a result started to explode the romantic tales of oppression. Lyons argued that he was seeking to break the 'Great Enchantment' which, at its most potent, has appeared to give historical legitimacy to the activities of modern paramilitary groups. Irish historians following this iconoclastic principle have been somewhat crudely dubbed 'revisionists' and, although the label is in some ways unhelpful, suggesting a dogmatic school of thought, it does give a useful name to a discernible historiographical tendency.

Despite the efforts of the revisionists, it remains true that the central theme of Anglo-Irish relations before the eighteenth century is one of the attempted, and only partially successful, conquest of Ireland by English and, to some extent, Scottish forces. The process began in 1171 with the invasion by the Norman king of England, Henry II, and the subsequent designation of Ireland as a lordship of the English Crown. But the Norman invaders were not only unable to subdue Ireland – famously controlling only the area around Dublin known as the Pale – but also became gradually assimilated into the indigenous culture such that after a few generations the Norman Irish were 'more Irish than the Irish'.

However, the outbreak of the Protestant Reformation in sixteenth-century Europe dramatically changed the nature of Anglo-Irish relations. Once the English Crown had drifted into the Protestant camp, albeit for expedient reasons, and Europe had begun its long slide into religious wars, the total conquest of Catholic Ireland and in particular the destruction of the power of the great Catholic chieftains and lords became both a religious and a strategic goal. Ireland must be ruled by reliable allies of the Crown and must therefore be Protestant. The subsequent period of 'Tudor Conquest' was unimaginably bloody. Though Elizabeth I could claim military victory after the crushing defeat of Ireland's Spanish allies at Kinsale in 1603, the expected Protestant Reformation in Ireland proved much harder to enforce.

Under James I a slightly more subtle policy was pursued. If the Irish would not become Protestants, then Protestants would be made Irish. To put it another way, the Crown would promote the settlement of Ireland by Protestants from England and Scotland. In this way Protestantism established certain areas of strength in the country such as parts of Ulster, an event with obvious long-term consequences. Many Catholics were forced off their land during this period.

The 'Tudor Conquest' and 'Stuart Plantation' inevitably provoked resistance and as a result Anglo-Irish relations in the seventeenth century were characterised by sporadic violence. The atrocities carried out by Catholics in 1641 and Cromwell's brutal reprisals in 1649, coupled with the grand Protestant epic of 1688–90 – when 'King Billy' (William III) fought and triumphed over the Catholic James II at the Boyne in 1690 – created enough martyrs to nourish several centuries of sectarian hatred. In many ways, for all the horrors of the Elizabethan wars, the seventeenth century remains the fertile seed-bed of continuing antagonisms. The modern marching season in Ulster is largely built around dates from the seventeenth century. The date of the battle of the Boyne, 12 July, is particularly sacred to the Orange Order, for example.

The defeat of James II at the Boyne has retrospectively come to be seen as the point at which the Catholic cause in Ireland was finally defeated. Thereafter there gradually emerged a clear Protestant ruling elite in Ireland, the Anglican aristocracy known as the Ascendancy. The rule of the Ascendancy was further buttressed by a collection of discriminatory laws, passed between 1690 and 1728, designed largely to suppress Catholicism.

The so-called penal laws imposed all manner of severe restrictions. Broadly, Catholics were excluded from all positions of power including Parliament. They were forbidden to buy land or inherit land from Protestants and their estates could not be passed on as a single property. In addition to that, the clergy were generally persecuted: bishops were banished from the country and ordinary priests forced to register and allowed to practise only in limited areas. In practice relatively few people were punished under this legislation but it did have the effect of forcing many of the landed Catholic families to convert to Anglicanism, thereby reinforcing the Ascendancy.

The social and sectarian structure of Ireland by the mid-eighteenth century was more complex than is usually allowed. Sandwiched awkwardly between the Ascendancy and the Catholic majority were the Presbyterians or Dissenters. The radicalism of the Nonconformist Protestant groups during the Cromwellian era had persuaded the English Crown to regard them as another threat to its security and for that reason the Irish Presbyterians, many of whom had acquired land in Ireland – especially in parts of Ulster – whilst fighting for the Crown, were also subject to legal discrimination under the penal laws. For this reason, the Dissenting Protestants proved to be at the very leading edge of the disturbances in the late eighteenth century. Indeed it was the growing community of interests between Dissenters and Catholics that made the non-sectarian ideology of revolutionary groups like the United Irishmen seem for a brief historical moment to make perfect political sense.

In broad social and economic terms, much of eighteenth-century Ireland was undergoing something of a boom, despite the various trade restrictions imposed from London. The population was expanding and even among the Catholics a commercial middle class was beginning to assert itself. But the fact that in many ways the Irish economy in the eighteenth century was flourishing only served to heighten the sense of injustice that many of the more economically successful groups, within both the Catholic and Dissenting communities, felt at their exclusion from political power.

But what perhaps gave the Anglo-Irish imperial relationship its strangest twist of all was the development of Irish national feeling amongst the Ascendancy. Despite being in descent from often brutally rapacious settlers, and despite the violent dislike of their fellow Irishmen further down the social scale, by the later eighteenth century the new generations of Irish aristocrats and country gentle-men had grown tired of the way the English government openly manipulated or simply bypassed the Irish Parliament. Taking inspiration from the rebellious attitudes of the American colonies in the 1760s, the so-called 'patriot' element among the Ascendancy elite began to take up the cause of Ireland whilst quietly overlooking the fact that the vast majority of Irishmen despised them. It was an odd sort of political double-think but nevertheless it alarmed the government. By the late 1770s the tensions, both within Ireland and between Ireland and England, were pushing matters towards a new breaking point.

1

REVOLUTIONS AND REACTIONS, 1775–1800

BACKGROUND NARRATIVE

Anglo-Irish relations in the later eighteenth century were transformed by the impact of two great external upheavals: the American War of Independence and the French Revolution.

The outbreak of revolt in the American colonies in 1775 was met with some sympathy in Ireland as both colonies resented the trade restrictions and high taxes imposed upon them from London. Politically the revolt strengthened the hand of a group of ambitious politicians in the Irish Parliament calling themselves 'the patriots'. This faction was led by Henry Grattan, who sought to use the crisis to extort greater rights for the Irish Parliament. As the crisis deepened and Britain found itself at war with France and Spain, the strategic position of Ireland, as a possible base for an invasion, began to give Irish demands a new urgency. This, coupled with the formation of local militias known as Volunteers, ostensibly designed to repel possible invaders, but potentially a threat to government forces, brought the Prime Minister, Lord North, to the conclusion that the time for concessions had arrived. In 1779 the right of free trade was granted to Irish companies, effectively removing many of the restrictions on Irish trade dating back to the Navigation Acts, and in 1782 the government granted what was called 'legislative independence' to the Irish Parliament. It appeared as though the patriots had won a great victory and the word 'independence' suggested that Ireland was now free to run its own affairs.

Historians have been at pains to point out that what became known as Grattan's Parliament did not have the power to govern Ireland independently. The royal Privy Council retained the right to overrule any legislation put forward in Dublin, all rights of appointment to senior positions remained in the hands of the government, and the Viceroy, also a royal appointee, was still the single most powerful man in Ireland. In many ways Grattan's Parliament was little different from the highly manipulated and wildly unrepresentative institution that existed before 1782. Nevertheless, in Anglo-Irish relations the important idea had been established, albeit more of a myth than a fact, that in 1782 Ireland had won the right to govern itself. This would be a touchstone for many Irish constitutional nationalists for the next century and more.

Yet Grattan and the gentlemen of the Irish upper classes were soon to be marginalised by the great historical wave emanating from France and rapidly sweeping across Europe. The French Revolution appeared to threaten the entire aristocratic order in Europe and consequently most of the patriots drifted back into a grudging loyalty to the old order. The government, in an attempt to ensure the wider loyalty of the Irish nation, decided to enfranchise the Catholic majority with the Catholic Relief Act of 1793, a doubly useful manoeuvre for the government in that it also threatened to further undermine patriot influence in the Irish Parliament.

The more significant impact of the French Revolution, however, was to be beyond the gilded world of Dublin high politics. French egalitarian ideas spread dangerously among those classes excluded from traditional political influence, namely the middling and lower classes, whether Protestant or Catholic, many of whom agreed that the time had come to check the powers of a corrupt and self-serving aristocracy. Nevertheless, what gave the revolution a particularly explosive impact in an Irish context was the stress on the idea of a people having rights to govern itself. In short, the Revolution preached a heady mix of egalitarianism and nationalism, both of which threatened to detonate the aristocratic framework binding the two nations.

The most famous Irish enthusiast for the French Revolution was one Theobald Wolfe Tone, a Protestant lawyer based in Belfast and a man usually seen as the father of separatist Irish nationalism. In 1791 he co-founded a group which was perhaps the first great republican organisation: the United Irishmen. In the same year he established a similar body in Dublin and gradually extended its network across the nation. Its aims were, to begin with, radical rather than revolutionary, calling for democracy in Ireland but not necessarily a complete break with the English Crown.

Inspired by the radicalisation of the Revolution in France in 1793, which had led to the execution of Louis XVI, Tone began to move towards more revolutionary ideas, a trend reinforced by Prime Minister Pitt's decision to declare the United Irishmen an illegal organisation.

In 1796 Tone travelled to France to seek its assistance in a proposed revolt against British rule in Ireland. He was successful. In 1796 the French sent a fleet of forty-three vessels with 14,450 soldiers on board, under the command of the renowned General Hoche, to Bantry Bay with the aim of linking up with the United Irishmen but after a disastrous storm only thirty-six vessels arrived, and due to adverse winds it was decided not to attempt a landing. Two years later Tone succeeded in organising a second French expedition which made a landing in County Mayo and achieved some success before government forces prevailed. In truth the rising had probably failed before it began. The army had begun a crackdown on the United Irishmen society after 1796 and once the fighting began it dealt with the rebels, and those wrongly suspected as rebels, with great ferocity. The suspension of Habeas Corpus and the declaration of martial law created a legal smokescreen behind which numerous massacres took place. The use of torture to extract information was also common, and the use of devices such as the pitch cap, a helmet of boiling tar to be forced upon the victim's head, was frequent enough.

The last battles, as at Vinegar Hill in June 1798, were more anticlimactic than heroic, as the rebel forces dissolved in the face of overwhelming odds. But the relative ease of the government's victory did not stop it from drawing the conclusion that there was something wrong with the way in which Ireland was governed. The need to obtain stronger and more reliable control of Ireland prompted Pitt to pass the Act of Union, as the result of which the Irish Parliament was closed down and Ireland was put under the direct rule of Westminster. The era of revolutions which had seemed to promise greater self-government for Ireland had ended in quite the opposite outcome.

ANALYSIS (1): HOW SIGNIFICANT WAS THE 1798 UPRISING?

It is hard to resist the view that the 1798 uprising must be of major significance if only because of the extraordinary levels of disruption and violence. Approximately 30,000 people were killed, many in cold blood, which makes the uprising the single most violent episode in modern Irish history: more people died in 1798 than in the infamously bloody civil war of 1922–3.

Inevitably the government found it extremely difficult to restore law and order. Local feuding continued and old scores continued to be settled well into the next century. The trials and sentencing dragged on until the end of the eighteenth century and in places like Wexford the sight of wretched men waiting on hulks for transportation to Australia created a mood of sullen resentment, all of which meant that the possibility of disorder hung over Anglo-Irish relations for the next generation or more.

As for the United Irishmen and the would-be revolutionary nationalists, it would be truer to say that rather than being simply defeated they retreated into secretive underground societies and plotted for the future. Perhaps the best example of the continued threat of nationalism came in 1803 with the failed uprising led by Robert Emmet. Although it was rather a doomed affair – Emmet led a poorly armed band of only 300 men against Dublin Castle – it nevertheless seemed to prove that the spirit of '98 would not be so easily crushed. Less concerned with ideologies, the British government saw the 1803 rising as just another example of the lack of respect for the law in Ireland, not an unreasonable conclusion given that during Emmet's rebellion the former Attorney General, General Arthur Wolfe, was dragged from his coach and piked to death. Emmet was sentenced to death but, like Tone, he was able to steal a sort of victory from the jaws of death. In his final speech in the courtroom Emmet requested that no man write his epitaph until his country be free, thereby passing on Tone's torch to subsequent generations.

Tone and Emmet were both engaged in rebellions that had little or no chance of success, although one cannot help wondering how the United Irishmen might have fared if the wind had changed when the French fleet stood off Bantry Bay in 1796. Nevertheless, through

the peculiar lens of Anglo-Irish relations, defeat can also be victory.
Tone had created an inspirational romantic role which generations of
nationalists proved extremely keen to play. Indeed, the entire insurrection created a kind of theme which would be played out again
and again over the next century, namely the power of the grand
gesture to overcome mere death.

In an ideological sense, although Tone by no means founded the
idea that Ireland was one nation, he fused this idea with the notion
of an independent republic in which Catholics and Protestants
would stand side by side. It is no accident, for example, that
modern nationalists venerate his name as the founder of republican
nationalism. Tone and the United Irishmen were perhaps the first
to fight for a modern concept of national independence. That said,
the fact remains that the rising failed. In order to grasp the deeper
significance of 1798 we must explore the reasons for its failure.

The most obvious reason is perhaps that, despite the name of the
United Irishmen, the Irish people were in fact deeply divided among
themselves. Tone had dreamt of a nationalism that would transcend
sectarian divisions: instead, the rising served to exacerbate those
very divisions. At Vinegar Hill, for example, the successful rebel
forces rounded up the Protestants of Enniscorthy and brutally
slaughtered them, often using pikes or scythes. In parts of Ulster
in 1797 the Orange Order enrolled in the loyalist yeomanry and militia
and set about terrorising entire Catholic communities and anyone
caught wearing green. In many cases the religious antagonisms
were interwoven with older family feuds which had little to do with
either politics or religion. Arguably, the long-established traditions
of banditry in Ireland, in which rival agrarian gangs waged incessant
turf wars, merely received legitimacy as old grievances were pursued
behind the cloak of a great rebellion.

Another related reason for the failure of the rebellion surely lies
in the fact that Toneite republicanism was, indirectly, the product
of the European Enlightenment, with its confident belief in reason
and contempt for ritualised, unthinking religious practices. As such
it was an urbane, intellectual outlook, unlikely to make much impact
upon the ordinary peasantry and rural workers. The works of Paine,
Rousseau or Voltaire made little headway in Ireland outside Belfast
and Dublin. Inevitably, perhaps, many of the peasantry remained
attached to their traditionally sectarian modes of thought.

In addition to the forces of religious tribalism, the rising was
also deeply fractured by class divisions and tensions. Some in the
Defender movement saw the war as a part of what might become a

Eco =
ↄ tithↄ
rats

National
Distinction)

few
core(n)

more social revolution, perhaps even leading to a more equal share of wealth. The Presbyterian Defender movement in Ulster began to call for wholesale land confiscation and redistribution, a radical slogan which served to alarm many of the more bourgeois members of the same movement. The leadership of the United Irishmen was largely middle class with a vested interest in maintaining the existing property arrangements. The sight of Irish workers urging Ireland to emulate some of the more extreme social policies of the Revolution in France only served to split the rebel movement.

On top of the religious and social divisions within the rebel movement there was also a generalised lack of organisation and little sense of national coordination. The whole insurrection was in truth a patchwork of disconnected actions which the authorities were able to deal with as such, rather than as one national rebellion. Ulster, for example, was perhaps the most radical province of all in 1796 and yet had all but been repressed before 1798 by the ferocious activities of Lieutenant-General Lake. In 1797 Lake proclaimed martial law and let loose a wave of house-burning, flogging and killing which smothered the Ulster movement a year before the south was ready to rise. As a result, when the peasantry of Kildare, Carlow and Wexford rose in the following year, the expected response from Ulster never came. Part of the reason for this lack of national coordination obviously lay in the crude nature of communications at the time but it is also true that for many of those involved in the fighting the grievances were of a local or provincial nature. Issues such as local rents or tithes could animate groups far more than the nationalist abstractions.

Against the argument that the rebel movement was fatally weakened by internal divisions it can argued that the British forces simply had superior weaponry and that the final outcome is merely a reflection of that underlying military reality. It is certainly true that many of the rebel units were armed only with home-made pikes, pitchforks, peat spades and all manner of working tools. The authorities, by contrast, could usually rely upon mobile artillery, rifles and pistols and a healthy line of supplies. All this is true but it must also be remembered that most of the governmental forces, and in particular the volunteer yeomanry, were themselves Irish. On 8 December 1797 Sir John Moore calculated that of the 76,791 fighting men available to the government in Ireland at that time, only 11,193 were English or Scottish, a calculation which, if correct, makes a mockery of Tone's belief in a United Ireland.

Evidently it is possible to see the 1798 rising as a confused, episodic fiasco hardly deserving of its mythic status. But this may be to miss the point. The divisions within Ireland were very real but this was still a seminal event. And for all the divisions and confusions the fact remains that large numbers of Irish men and women had begun to talk in republican terms and indeed taken up arms for their country. Although the movement was not centrally organised and lacked any sense of an overall strategy, it is nevertheless true that the United Irishmen had laid the basis of a national network. Right across Ireland, with the possible exception of the far west, the United Irishmen had made connections. In some respects it may be possible to see the rising as the beginning of a process of politicisation: a slow awakening of national consciousness. The numbers of people tortured or murdered created a rich legacy of tales of martyrdom which in themselves further developed a sense of national consciousness. Ordinary men and women, such as the farmer William Orr, made passionate gallows speeches invoking the love of their country. The numerous injustices involved in the governmental crackdown only served to amplify the emotional volume of such oratory; the balladeers and bards did the rest. Revisionist historians will always stress that the rising reveals just how exceptionally weak non-sectarian nationalism was and how divided along class lines Georgian Ireland was, and further argue that the entire event was a retrogressive development, leading as it did to the closure of the Irish Parliament. But on the other hand, there can be no doubt that the failed insurrection stamped an idea of an independent republic into the minds of Irishmen for generations to come. In that sense, as so often in Anglo-Irish relations, it was not what happened that mattered but what people thought had happened.

Questions

1. Discuss the view that Irish society was divided in too many ways to support an effective uprising in 1798.
2. What, if anything, did Wolfe Tone achieve?
3. How true is it to say that in 1798 England suppressed an Irish nationalist uprising?

ANALYSIS (2): WHY WAS THE ACT OF UNION PASSED AND WHAT WERE THE CONSEQUENCES?

The Act of Union of 1800 created a United Kingdom of Great Britain and Ireland: a kingdom legislated for by one Parliament in London. The Irish Parliament which had met, in one form or another, intermittently during the previous five hundred years was abolished.

The main reason for this development was clear: the 1798 rebellion had so shocked the British government that it was felt that a more reliable and effective system of control was necessary. The fact that Britain remained at war with revolutionary France in 1799 only served to increase the sense that Ireland was a political and strategic weak point. In fact this line of thinking had been almost a consistent theme in the discussions of the Cabinet ever since the American War had first raised the spectre of revolution. By 1799 there was a clear majority at Westminster in favour of removing the assembly that had all too clearly failed to keep order; it was judged on its past record to be not only weak but also politically fickle. In that sense Pitt and his government were passing judgement upon the Irish Parliament for its opportunism in 1782 as well as its failures in 1798.

In addition to political and strategic considerations there was, as ever, an undertow of racial feeling: the Act emerged from the kind of thinking which argued that the lawless Irish people were not fit to have a Parliament of their own. Such prejudices were not always aimed at the poor Catholic peasantry; the Act was in a real sense a reflection of the English aristocracy's exasperation with their Irish counterparts. The Ascendancy had been judged an inferior elite.

However, the Irish Parliament was not simply closed down against the wishes of the Irish MPs. Rather, the government had to persuade the Irish Parliament to abolish itself. Pitt delegated this delicate task to the English Lord Lieutenant of Ireland, Lord Cornwallis. The Lord Lieutenant was not enthusiastic, describing it as a job of 'the most unpleasant nature'.[1] It was not that the Parliamentarians resisted but rather that they demanded a high price for their support, hence Cornwallis described them as 'the most corrupt people under heaven'.[2] As a result Cornwallis duly delegated the distasteful business of purchasing the necessary votes to the Chief Secretary, Lord Castlereagh. The first attempt at a Union bill was rejected by two votes, but then Castlereagh began to get to work on the Opposition. Die-hard opponents such as John Foster, the Irish Chancellor of the

Exchequer, were stripped of their office, whilst most were bought off with pensions, positions or peerages. Although it should be stressed that such 'management' of Parliament was fairly normal by eighteenth-century standards, the idea gradually took hold afterwards that Britain had effectively bribed away the ancient assembly of Ireland.

In reality the dissolution of the Irish Parliament did not provoke popular discontent. Partly this was because Pitt had promised that the Act of Union would go hand in hand with an Act of Catholic Emancipation. As a result, many Catholics, who had little or no sympathy with the entirely Protestant Parliament in Dublin, felt that their interests might be served more effectively by supporting the idea of Union. In the event, King George III blocked the enactment of Catholic Emancipation, an action which in due course only served to accelerate the emergence of a movement for Emancipation. The collapse of the Emancipation initiative still did not provoke serious hostility to the Act of Union. Most of the Irish Parliamentarians, including John Foster, were staunchly anti-Catholic and so there was little or no chance of any kind of political alliance forming against the Union. Though there were a few English MPs and peers who resented the Irish 'invasion' of Westminster, the Parliament in London voted through this major change in the constitution with an attitude bordering on casualness. It was decided, in a rather ad hoc way, that Ireland should have a hundred MPs and twenty-eight peers, with a further four Irish bishops from the Church of Ireland in the Lords.

The way in which the Act had been hastily thrown together left all sorts of matters unresolved. At first the Irish Exchequer in Dublin was to continue, thereby creating some confusion about taxation and the whole financing of government policy in Ireland. The two exchequers were eventually merged in 1817 and the two tax systems broadly standardised. Nevertheless, there was always a confusion about the exact relationship between the representatives in London and the Lord Lieutenant and Chief Secretary in Dublin. The day-to-day political governance of Ireland reverted to the Castle and in many ways the Lord Lieutenant expanded his role into that of an Imperial Viceroy, the personal symbol of the British Empire, in a colony now almost more distant than before. But in other ways Irish MPs at Westminster now found themselves much closer to the real centres of power. Thus there was an ambiguity about the Act: in a legal constitutional sense Ireland had become an integrated part of the most powerful kingdom in the world, but in terms of symbols and national pride the Act seemed to involve a lessening of national prestige.

There were, however, some undoubted gains for Ireland as a result of the Act. The Protestants of the commercial middling classes, who had feared that the Act might empower the Catholics, were appeased by the fact that not only was Catholic Emancipation not part of the package, but the United Kingdom was also to be turned into a free trade area, which promised great benefits for the Belfast linen industry in particular. Many of the former politicians in Dublin, such as Grattan and Foster, were able to continue their careers in the new setting. In the slightly longer term it has been argued that the British government, in its efforts to make the Union work, was rather more generous to Ireland than to other parts of the United Kingdom; certainly the state intervened in Irish domestic affairs, in areas such as education and public health, in ways which arguably put Ireland ahead of the mainland. All manner of initiatives that eventually became law in England were often tested first in Ireland: the best example being perhaps the police force.

More negatively, nationalists have tended to see such state meddling as evidence that the government in London chose to use Ireland as a conveniently distant location for social experimentation. No matter how one interprets government policy towards Ireland after the Act of Union, there can be no doubt that by bringing Irish MPs into Westminster the British government had given Irish politicians the ability to make Irish issues far more central than they had previously been.

In order to grasp this change it is important to look at both the short- and long-term significance of the Act. At first, it was not apparent that the Act had in any way strengthened the hand of nationalists. Despite the fact that Grattan delivered a few passionate speeches in Westminster against the Act he was largely a spent force and most of the imported MPs were the loyal placemen of the existing order. However, in the longer term and particularly after O'Connell eventually won Catholic Emancipation in 1829, the government gradually awoke to the fact that Catholic and/or nationalist Irish MPs could now use Westminster as a forum for their ideas. As the nineteenth century unfolded and leaders such as O'Connell and later Parnell began using the situation to paralyse the British political process, the Act must have come to look less like a practical solution and more like the root of all Anglo-Irish difficulties.

What made these problems particularly galling, from the government's perspective, was the feeling that despite having unwittingly given Ireland the opportunity to put itself at the top of the British agenda, there was always the myth, wonderfully exploited by O'Connell and especially Parnell, that England had robbed the Irish people of their ancient Parliament. The fact that the vast majority of Irishmen were not sorry to see the Irish Parliament disappear at the time was generally overlooked. In a curious way the government had achieved the worst of both worlds: casting themselves as oppressors ruling Ireland through a dictatorial Viceroy and yet managing to give Ireland the means to make Parliamentary life as difficult as possible.

In the late Victorian and Edwardian periods the Act took on an exceptional, even iconic, status, way beyond anything dreamt of in 1800. For nationalists the removal of the Act and the restitution of a Parliament – what was known as the campaign for Home Rule – became a grand cause and one which convulsed British political life to the extent that it was almost responsible for the destruction of the Liberal Party. For these Home Rule nationalists the Act was pictured as the legislative manacle that must be cast off. But for Protestants, particularly the Presbyterian men of the north, this Act – about which they had been so sceptical in 1800 – came to be referred to as a semi-sacred guarantee of their freedoms and continued existence.

In conclusion, in 1799 Pitt had sought a way to defuse Anglo-Irish tensions and bring Ireland into a new unitary kingdom but instead he had only succeeded in making Anglo-Irish relations more intractable than ever.

Questions

1. Why was the Act of Union introduced?
2. How true is to say that in 1800 England robbed Ireland of its Parliament?
3. Why was there so little resistance to the passing of the Act of Union?

SOURCES

1. CONSTITUTIONAL AND REVOLUTIONARY UPHEAVAL, 1782–98

Source A: Henry Grattan's speech to the Irish Parliament on the eve of 'legislative independence' in 1782.

I am now to address a free people. Ages have passed away, and this is the first moment in which you could be distinguished by that appellation. I have spoken on the subject of your liberty so often that I have nothing to add, and have only to admire by what heaven directed steps you have proceeded until the whole faculty of the nation is braced up to the act of her own deliverance. I found Ireland on her knees; I watched over her with a paternal solicitude; I have traced her progress from injuries to arms, and from arms to Liberty. Spirit of Swift, spirit of Molyneux, your genius has prevailed. Ireland is now a nation.

Source B: From the 'dying declaration' of William Orr, a Protestant sympathiser with the United Irishmen, executed in 1797.

My comfortable lot and industrious course of life, best refute the charge of being adventurer for plunder; but if to have loved my country, to have known its wrongs, to have felt the injuries of the persecuted Catholic, and to have united with them and all other religious persons in the most orderly and least sanguinary means of procuring redress – if these be felonies, I am a felon, but not otherwise.

Source C: From *The Autobiography of Theobald Wolfe Tone, 1763–1798*, posthumously published in 1893.

Animated by their unconquerable hatred of France, which no change of circumstance could alter, the whole English nation, it may be said, retracted from their first decision in favour of the glorious and successful efforts of the French people; they sickened at the prospect of approaching liberty and happiness of that mighty nation: they calculated as merchants, the probable effects which the energy of regenerated France might have on their commerce . . . But matters were different in Ireland, an oppressed, insulted and plundered nation. As we well knew, experimentally, what it was to be enslaved, we sympathised most sincerely with the French people. As the Revolution advanced, and as events expanded themselves, the public spirit of Ireland rose with a rapid acceleration. The fears and animosities of the aristocracy rose in the same, or a still higher proportion. In a little time the French Revolution became the test of every man's political creed.

Source D: From a pastoral address by John Thomas Troy, Roman Catholic Archbishop of Dublin (1798).

At present when these kingdoms are seriously menaced with invasion by a formidable and implacable enemy, when too many have been seduced into a persuasion that French Republicans are our friends and allies, desirous to fraternise with us, for the sole purpose of delivering us from bondage, and securing our religion and liberty, I cannot be silent . . .

Compare your present situation with the past. Twenty years ago the exercise of your religion was prohibited by law. You are now at liberty to profess your religion openly and practise the duties of it. A college [Maynooth Seminary] for the education of your clergy has been erected at the recommendation of his Majesty and the restraints upon your industry have been removed.

You will perhaps reply, that some legal disabilities still exclude the most loyal and peaceable Roman Catholics from a seat or a vote in Parliament, from the Privy Council, from the higher and confidential civil and military departments of the state. I grant it. But, is it by rebellion, insurrection, tumult or seditious clamour on your part, that these incapacities are to be removed? Most certainly not.

Source E: From an address by General Napper Tandy, of the United Irish army, to his fellow countrymen (1798, also dated 'from the first year of Irish Liberty').

Horrid crimes have been perpetrated in your country. Your friends have fallen a sacrifice to their devotion for your cause. Their shadows err around you and call aloud for Vengeance. It is your duty to avenge their death. It is your duty to strike on their blood cemented thrones, the murderers of your friends. Listen to no proposals Irish men, wage a war of extermination against your oppressors, the war of Liberty against Tyranny and Liberty shall triumph.

Questions

1. Explain what Tandy meant in Source E when he spoke of 'shadows' that 'call aloud for Vengeance'. (3 marks)
*2. What criticism might be made of Grattan's assessment, in Source A, of Ireland's status in 1782? (5 marks)

3. Explain how the United Irishmen might have made use of Orr's speech (Source B) in their propaganda campaigns. (5 marks)
4. Compare Sources C and D. How far do they differ in their attitude towards the idea of revolution? (12 marks)

Worked answer

*2. In many respects Grattan is guilty of a level of exaggeration bordering on fiction. Ireland was not a 'free people' in 1782 any more than it had been before. Ireland had not become 'a nation' or risen off its knees to 'liberty'. The granting of 'legislative independence' was in truth only the smallest of concessions which changed little. The Privy Council retained the right to overturn any Irish legislation, the government controlled all appointments and the executive power remained in the hands of the Lord Lieutenant, again a crown appointment. In addition to these constitutional barriers, there was the more pervasive impediment to meaningful self-government: the fact that Georgian politics was if anything more prone to the pressures of jobbery and bribery than the so-called 'Old Corruption' of Westminster. This point is illustrated all too clearly in the relatively smooth way in which the Irish Parliamentarians were 'persuaded' to abolish themselves in 1800. It might be added that the allegedly 'free nation', outside Dublin, made little or no protest at this pulling down of the supposed bastion of their liberties. In truth the vast majority of Irish men and women, including Catholics and Presbyterians, regarded the College Green assembly with either hostility, suspicion or indifference. Inevitably then one is bound to agree with Professor Foster's verdict that 'the reality of 1782 was largely cosmetic: an effect brought about by Grattan's speeches'.

But Grattan was not being entirely literal. The freedom he championed was the freedom of his class: the Ascendancy; and for a brief historical moment there was a sense that the Irish landed elite had scored a significant small victory over their English social rivals. Indeed, within the glittering world of such arrogant gentlemen, their little social triumphs could all too easily be recast as victories for the whole nation. However, the idea that Grattan spoke for all of Ireland was largely rhetorical sleight of hand. In fact, of course, the emergence of mass politics in the nineteenth century would rapidly destroy the Ascendancy as a political force.

SOURCES

2. THE CONSEQUENCES OF THE 1798 RISING

Source F: From King George III's speech against the idea of Catholic Emancipation (June 1798).

There can be only one national church, whose members must therefore have a monopoly of government, and no country can be governed where there is more than one established religion; the others may be tolerated, but that cannot extend further than leave to perform their religious duties according to the tenets of their church.

Source G: From the correspondence of the Lord Lieutenant, Lord Cornwallis (June 1799).

My occupation is now of the most unpleasant nature, negotiating and jobbing with the most corrupt people under heaven. I despise and hate myself every hour for engaging in such dirty work, and am supported only by the reflection that without a Union the British Empire must be dissolved . . .

Source H: From Patrick Pearse's commemorative address at the grave of Wolfe Tone in 1913. (Pearse was later executed for his part in the Easter Rising of 1916.)

We have come to the holiest place in Ireland; holier than the place where St. Patrick sleeps in Down. Patrick brought us life, but this man died for us. He was the greatest of Irish nationalists. We have come to renew our adhesion to the faith of Tone: to express once more our full acceptance of the gospel of Irish nationalism which he was first to formulate in worldly terms. This man's soul was a burning flame, so pure that to come into communion with it is to come unto a new baptism, into a new regeneration and cleansing.

Source I: From *The Evolution of Irish Nationalist Politics* by Tom Garvin (Dublin: Gill & Macmillan, 1981).

The early United Irishmen, moving out from Belfast and Dublin into the villages and the countryside in their search for popular support, found themselves attempting to combine Catholic and Protestant elements at a time when the sectarian gap was widening . . . As the movement spread, it came under the influence of its own rank and file, who elected leaders who thought like themselves rather than like the middle class *philosophes* of Dublin or Belfast.

Source J: Adapted extract from 'Remembering 1798' published in *The Irish Story* by R.F. Foster (London: Penguin, 2001).

The subsequent historiography embodied fixed positions of partisanship. The historical treatments of the rising set hard into orthodoxy during the nineteenth century. From the Unionist side, it was a bloodthirsty religious war for the expropriation of Protestants, led by priests and fuelled by memories of the seventeenth century. However, writers like Tom Moore had early on established the nobility of the enterprise. For the radical nationalist tradition (at least from the growth of the Young Ireland movement in the late 1830s, and further bolstered by the Fenian journalism of the 1860s), 1798 was a heroic rising against oppression.

Questions

1. Explain the references in Source F to the following:
   (i) 'established religion'. (2 marks)
   (ii) 'monopoly of government'. (2 marks)
*2. How useful is Source I to a historian studying the reasons for the failure of the 1798 rising? (6 marks)
3. Explain why Lord Cornwallis (Source G) felt that he must do business with 'corrupt' people. (4 marks)
4. What do Sources H and J tell you about the way the history of 1798 has been used for propaganda purposes by differing groups in Ireland? (11 marks)

Worked answer

*2. Source I is very useful as an analysis of the reasons for the failure of the rising because it highlights the two key internal problems within the rebel movement, namely class tensions and sectarian differences. As Garvin points out, the movement was broadly split between a lower-class 'rank and file' and a middle-class leadership. As the cause sought to spread beyond Dublin and Belfast it came increasingly under the influence of the poorer classes. The rank and file, we can assume to have been largely from the peasantry, particularly as Garvin stresses the fact that the divide between classes was also that between town and country. But the problem was about more than mere class; it was about the way people from different social groups thought. The *philosophes* were a group of middle-

and upper-class intellectuals, such as Voltaire and Rousseau, often credited with having created the ideas which inspired the French Revolution. To say that the rebels rejected the ideas of the 'middle class *philosophes* of Dublin and Belfast' is to imply both that the rebels were not inspired by the ideals of the French Revolution and also that the peasants rejected such ideals on class lines: as Garvin says, the rural rebels chose people who 'thought like themselves'. The mental outlook of the rank and file was profoundly sectarian, hence the ideology of the revolutionary movement became confused and ultimately returned to the traditional religious mould of much older conflicts. This sort of ideological confusion helps to explain not only the eventual failure of the rising but also the disturbing counter-narrative of visceral sectarian atrocity which lies behind the myths of 1798.

In many ways, then, the source does illuminate the internal contradictions within the allegedly Republican side. But of course there are limits to the utility of the source. A number of factors which help to explain the failure are not touched upon in any way: for example, the superior arms of the government forces, the lack of communications between the rebel groups and the resultant lack of coordination, the peculiar geographical dispersal of the fighting, the failure of the French to make the landing in 1796 and, of course, the sheer brutality of the government forces. Nevertheless, any historian assessing the failure of 1798 would find Garvin's views absolutely central to any overall explanation.

2

THE AGE OF THE LIBERATOR, 1800–45

BACKGROUND NARRATIVE

The Act of Union closed the Irish Parliament in Dublin and was therefore routinely denounced by all manner of Irish nationalists. But oddly it was this Act which actually made a genuine Irish nationalist politics possible, by transferring Irish issues from the relative margin of Dublin to the main focus point of British political life: Westminster. It is perhaps an additional irony that the manner of the passing of the Act also provided Irish politicians with a ready-made cause, namely Catholic Emancipation.

Throughout the 1790s the British government had been busy making concessions to Catholics in order, in effect, to buy their support during the war against revolutionary France. Prime Minister Pitt intended to sweeten, and indeed strengthen, the Union by abolishing the seventeenth-century laws which prevented Catholics from becoming MPs or holding any number of civil and governmental offices. In the event King George III and the House of Lords conspired to remove the emancipatory clauses from the legislation that established the Union. Hence, with its passing, Catholic expectations were dashed and a great campaign was born.

All successful campaigns need effective leaders. In Daniel O'Connell Ireland found a leader of exceptional gifts: a hard-headed Catholic barrister with a talent for abusive oratory (a talent that led him into several duels), a radical liberal's passion for the rights of underdogs and, above all, a theatrical talent for what might be called gestural politics.

After several failed attempts to push an Emancipation bill through Parliament, O'Connell hit upon a new strategy: the mobilisation of the Catholic majority. In 1823 he formed the Catholic Association, and invited all ordinary Catholics to join for a small fee, known as the 'Catholic rent'. The church itself provided the necessary organisational framework upon which to hang this new movement, despite the misgivings of many of the senior Catholic bishops. Having created what was probably the first genuine mass protest movement in British political history, he then aimed this bandwagon at the sacred Anglican constitution.

It must also be said that there were clear signs that by 1828 the British Prime Minister, Wellington, was moving reluctantly to the conclusion that emancipation was inevitable. The repeal of the Test and Corporation Acts in 1828, which removed restrictions on Nonconformists, was a clear signal that the seventeenth century might be over.

O'Connell's moment arrived with the promotion of the Conservative Vesey Fitzgerald, sitting member for County Clare, to the Cabinet. In those days this necessitated a by-election and O'Connell decided to stand, an action not in itself illegal despite the bar on Catholics taking up a seat. Unsurprisingly, given the guaranteed vote of the members of the Catholic Association, he won, thereby creating a crisis. As O'Connell said, 'they must now crush us or conciliate us'.[1] The former policy would undoubtedly have led to a wave of disturbances in Ireland. It would also have been costly to enforce.

Wellington and his Home Secretary, Robert Peel, contrived a clever double-edged solution: concede to the Catholics in such a way as simultaneously to undermine O'Connell's power base. This they did in 1829 by passing a Catholic Relief Act which opened most but not all doors to Catholics (to this day a Catholic is not eligible for the English throne) but which also dramatically reduced the electorate in Ireland by raising the county franchise from 40 shillings to £10. The county electorate shrank from 216,000 to 37,000. This robbed O'Connell of much of his electorate and sharply diminished the political power of the Catholic Association.

After the triumph of Emancipation O'Connell took his place as an MP and gradually put together an O'Connellite party of thirty or so.

The Great Reform Act of 1832 did little for Ireland except to increase the number of Irish representatives by five. Nevertheless, Ireland, largely thanks to O'Connell's rhetorical assaults on the Union, remained central to British politics throughout the 1830s and 1840s. The Whigs, in power for most of the 1830s, sought to appease Irish opinion and generally pacify the country by introducing a number of progressive reforms such as the Education Act of 1831 which established the first state-funded primary schools anywhere in Britain. The Irish Church Temporalities Act of 1833 abolished ten Anglican bishoprics in Ireland, thereby in small measure reducing the financial burden on the Irish to support what was, for most, an alien church.

O'Connell gave guarded support to these measures and was even prepared to enter into an alliance with the Whigs, the so-called Lichfield House Compact of 1835, to keep them in power, and the more aggressively Protestant Tory Party out. But by 1840 it became apparent to O'Connell that the Whigs had no intention of supporting his next major project: repeal of the Act of Union. The emerging Repeal movement was a campaign, in effect, for a restored Irish Parliament in Dublin.

The Repeal campaign was financed in the same sort of way as the Emancipation campaign, with a Repeal 'rent'. Again, the Roman Catholic Church provided its backing. O'Connell also had the support of a band of youthful middle-class intellectuals calling themselves 'Young Ireland'. In addition to that, he also had the continuing devotion of most of the poor peasantry, with the exception of Ulster. The main tactic this time was the organisation of 'monster meetings': huge gatherings designed to intimidate the English government by sheer weight of numbers. According to O'Connell's rhetoric at least, these crowds were to remain peaceable and well intentioned, thus making it very difficult for the authorities to suppress them.

The movement began in 1840 but in 1841 the Tories returned to power, with Peel as Prime Minister. Peel was not inclined to concede to O'Connell again – his own reputation as defender of Protestants (hence his nickname 'Orange Peel') having taken quite a bruising after Catholic Emancipation. Unlike the Whigs, Peel was not in any way dependent upon the O'Connellite group in the House and there is also no doubt that the two men disliked each other on a purely personal level. Indeed, they had come very close to fighting a duel only a few years before.

The Repeal issue came to a head in 1843 when O'Connell proposed another monster meeting at Clontarf. Peel, having steadily built up the strength of the army in Ireland over the two previous years, decided to ban the proposed meeting. Faced with the prospect of breaking the law in a way that would undoubtedly lead to widespread violence and probable loss of life, O'Connell climbed down and accepted the ban. This defeat signalled, in effect, the beginning of the end of the Repeal movement. Furthermore, Peel pressed his advantage home quite ruthlessly. In 1844 O'Connell was arrested for language judged to be an incitement to violence. Although it would be an exaggeration to say that prison broke O'Connell, there can be little doubt that the impact of this experience upon the 69-year-old politician left him significantly sapped and demoralised.

Over the next two years, O'Connell's apparent weakness was coupled with quarrels within the Repeal movement, and Peel's continuing policy of combating Repeal with concessions, such as the increased grant to Maynooth College (the main seminary for training Catholic clergy In Ireland). These factors all combined to derail the movement completely.

Though it may not have been apparent in 1846, when Peel fell from power both men were spent forces. O'Connell died in 1847 and Peel only three years later. Nevertheless, despite their bitter rivalry, between them they had achieved much for Ireland and indeed for Anglo-Irish relations. But their legislative accomplishments and their overall legacy were to be set into a particularly unforgiving context as the slow tragedy of the Great Famine began to unfurl itself after 1845.

ANALYSIS (1): WHY DID O'CONNELL SUCCEED IN EMANCIPATING THE CATHOLICS BUT NOT IN REPEALING THE ACT OF UNION?

The success of the Emancipation campaign was due to a unique conjunction of factors. First and foremost was the deliberate harnessing of the power of the Catholic Church to the political movement for

Emancipation. This was O'Connell's great achievement. The Roman Catholic Church functioned as a ready-made organisational structure; church services could be both an occasion to pay the 'Catholic rent' and hear the message direct from the pulpit. In politicising the Catholic Church O'Connell mobilised the biggest single institution in Ireland. The weight of numbers was crucial in the election of 1828. It was the sheer size of the movement which made it a phenomenon which the government was unwilling to meet head on.

However, despite the church's similar role in the collecting of a 'Repeal rent', its role in the Repeal campaign was far less effective. The main reason for this was that it was not an issue that could be defined in narrow confessional terms. Repeal was intended for all Irishmen, Catholic, Anglican and Dissenter alike. Hence in some ways priests could almost serve to alienate sections of the movement. Conversely, if it was presented as a secular constitutional issue the church tended to shy away from it as something smacking a little too much of European liberalism, an ideology widely regarded by Catholics as dangerously prone to godlessness. O'Connell tried hard to square this circle but never really shook off the image of being primarily a leader of Catholics. It is noteworthy that Ulster contributed very little indeed to O'Connell's movement. It might even be argued that O'Connell damaged the cause of Irish nationalism by forging the bond between it and Catholicism rather too effectively.

Ironically O'Connell was not in favour of a confessional nationalism and argued along good liberal lines for a complete severance of church and state. However, his victory in 1829 sealed the bond between his name and the Catholic cause. It should also be added that many of the middle-class Catholics who championed O'Connell in 1829 were a little more uneasy about the idea of Repeal because it was unclear how this might affect trade and the Irish economy in general. There were many who saw the Union in such commercial terms, as a useful connection with the most powerful economic empire in the world. Nationalists preferred to argue that the Irish economy suffered as a result of being shackled to British interests.

It was not only along sectarian and economic lines that the movement felt a certain uneasiness with itself. There were also underlying criticisms of O'Connell's leadership stemming from the more impatient members of the Young Ireland movement. Despite the fact that O'Connell had nurtured the Young Ireland leaders, such as Duffy, Davis and Mitchel, it gradually became clear that they were nationalists of a very different sort. The most obvious difference was the fact that they were mainly from Protestant backgrounds.

This created a little friction in itself but more importantly their out-look owed more to European Romantic nationalism, such as that espoused by Herder and Mazzini, than to the more pragmatic liberal nationalism of O'Connell. In practice this led to sharply different ideas about strategy. O'Connell always opted for legal protest, partly because he thought uprisings futile, but the Young Irelanders gradually came to favour physical force. Futility, in the sense of certain defeat, for a Romantic nationalist is precisely the point.

Given the ardour of Young Ireland, it is hardly surprising that O'Connell's climb-down over the Clontarf meeting effectively split the movement into warring camps and thereby fatally weakened it. It might be thought odd that a man who had killed another in a duel, as O'Connell certainly had, would be steadfastly non-violent. The answer to this apparent conundrum is that O'Connell was a gentleman and as such felt obliged to obey Dublin society's codes of behaviour, such as duelling. In a political context his aversion to violence can be traced back to the fact that he had been in school in France during the French Revolution – an experience which cured him of any naive romanticism about the nature of revolutions: hard experience which most of the men of Young Ireland conspicu-ously lacked.

It is easy to pillory Young Ireland as rather foolish, for example by highlighting the stupidity of advocating a rejection of English and a return to Gaelic when none of the leaders could speak it. Para-doxically, O'Connell was fluent in the Irish language but felt that English was the preferable language for a modernising Ireland.

There is, however, a serious question mark about O'Connell's strategies in seeking to persuade the government to take the idea of Repeal seriously. It is hard to see how O'Connell felt that big meetings in Ireland would have much effect in London. By totally rejecting physical force options and in particular in rejecting the rhetoric of revolution, which was the real preference of Young Ireland, O'Connell left himself with very little with which to bargain. Increasingly, this fact became obvious.

In addition to the paucity of strategies, one must also give some weight to the simple matter of O'Connell's age during the Repeal campaign. He was sixty-nine when he was sent to prison in 1844. 'Prison' actually turned out to be a fairly comfortable spell of house arrest, with attendant servants and resident wife and family; nevertheless it remains true that after 1844 he simply lacked the physical energy to make all the slow and often uncomfortable journeys necessary to maintain the momentum of the Repeal campaign. It might also be conjectured that the row with Young Ireland was also in some ways simply the impatience of youth with old age.

It has been suggested that O'Connell should have sought an alliance with the Chartists, who were also calling for major constitutional reform. However, O'Connell was deeply suspicious of the Chartist leader Feargus O'Connor, not least because O'Connor was an unstable personality, much given to empty threats of revolution. Given O'Connell's canny instincts and his attitude to political violence, it is hardly surprising that the two bandwagons remained on very different trajectories, united only in the end by their respective failures.

More important than any of these considerations was the English political context in which O'Connell was operating. In the Emancipation campaign O'Connell was distinctly aided by the fact that the idea of Emancipation had been in circulation for some time before 1828 and was widely accepted as sensible among elements of both parties. It might well be argued that it had been on the agenda since the 1790s when concessionary politics was the name of the game. Indeed Pitt's original intention to bolt Emancipation into the Act of Union positively ensured that it would be a big issue when the Act turned out otherwise. In 1826 a bill calling for emancipation of Catholics passed through the Commons and only failed due to a combination of royal string-pulling and the Protestant bloc in the Lords. O'Connell therefore merely had to find a way of pressing the issue. This he did in the by-election of 1829 and even men as distinctly 'Orange' as Peel and Wellington could not find the political will to oppose it.

The idea of Repeal, however, received no such favourable winds; indeed it spent most of the 1830s becalmed as neither major party showed any interest in it. The radicals on the left of the Whigs, from whom O'Connell could normally expect sympathy, found the issue unappealing. The imagined spectacle of Britain conceding a legislature to what might be seen as a colony was too dangerous a precedent even for most radicals. The concessions that the Whigs did give to Ireland, such as the Education Act, the Irish Church Temporalities Act and the Irish Tithe Commutation Act, were given precisely as a means of demonstrating the benign nature of the British government of Ireland under the Act of Union. Despite the five years of the Lichfield House Compact, O'Connell was never able to move the Whigs any closer to the notion of Repeal.

To some extent his impotence can be traced back to Peel's sweeping reduction of the size of the Irish electorate in 1829 and the fact that the 1832 Reform Act only marginally redressed the situation. (Ireland would have to wait until the 1884 Reform Act before an Irish electorate became large enough for the nationalists to form a mass political movement again.) The O'Connellite party at Westminster always remained too small to get its hand on any serious levers of influence. Worse still, the 1841 election created a majority Tory government under O'Connell's old adversary Robert Peel.

When Peel became Prime Minister in 1841 O'Connell must surely have known that it was a result which virtually guaranteed the failure of the Repeal movement. Put crudely, Peel and O'Connell hated each other. Peel had already been forced into the relative humiliation of Emancipation by O'Connell and was hardly likely to allow a similar débâcle to occur. Furthermore, the election of 1841 gave the Conservatives a clear majority and therefore no need to horse-trade with any political faction. But what made Peel such a powerful opponent was not so much personal animosity as the fact that Peel had come to believe wholeheartedly in the Union and was taking positive steps to strengthen the tie. Peel's policy towards Ireland was one of deliberate concession to respectable middle-class Catholic opinion, most famously by tripling the grant to the major training college for Catholic priests, Maynooth Seminary. The more Peel pursued this line, the harder it became for O'Connell to paint the Union as a negative arrangement which somehow deprived Ireland of good government. In short, to some extent it can be said that Peel killed Repeal with kindness.

In conclusion, it is apparent that the arrangement of political parties and factions in the 1840s simply gave O'Connell nothing with which to bargain. No matter how he defined and redefined what Repeal might mean – oddly the Irish Parliament that O'Connell was calling for remained in detail undefined throughout the campaign in terms both of how it was to be elected and of what powers it was to enjoy – there were no takers. The irony in all this is that to some extent O'Connell was the victim of his own success. Catholic Emancipation restored credibility to the Union in Catholic eyes. In some ways O'Connell had unwittingly forced Peel to restore to the Union the very selling point that Pitt had intended. Not only that, he seemed to have pointed Peel in the direction of a concession-based Unionism that would make the British government seem relatively benign. As a result O'Connell found it increasingly difficult to depict the government in London as being indifferent to Irish grievances. Thus, although numerous factors determined the failure of Repeal, there is much truth in the idea that success in 1829 virtually guaranteed failure thereafter.

Questions

1. How did O'Connell succeed in forcing the British government to introduce Catholic Emancipation?
2. Why did O'Connell fail to work effectively with either the Young Ireland movement or the Chartists?

ANALYSIS (2): HOW SUCCESSFUL WAS PEEL IN HIS HANDLING OF IRISH AFFAIRS BEFORE 1845?

Peel's name was first associated with Ireland in 1809 when his father arranged for him to represent the rotten borough of Cashel in Tipperary: a not particularly unusual twenty-first birthday present for a self-made industrialist to give an undoubtedly brilliant son. It seems that Peel had no inherent interest in the place at that point in his career but that Cashel just happened to be a convenient door through which to enter Parliament.

In 1812, however, Lord Liverpool elevated Peel by appointing him Chief Secretary for Ireland, a very promising rung on the career ladder but nevertheless a demanding post. Peel faced two major problems whilst Chief Secretary. First was the endemic lawlessness and violence associated with the phenomenon normally described as 'Whiteboyism' or 'Ribbonism'. The Whiteboys were in fact a rural band of ruffians, often sporting white bandanas or ribbons, who usually used intimidatory violence against property and livestock to 'negotiate' with landlords who seemed to be charging unreasonable rents or evicting tenants. By the time of Peel's secretaryship the Whiteboys themselves were a thing of the past but any number of similar bands – with names like The Whitefeet, The Threshers, The Rockites and so forth – had proliferated, helping to earn for Ireland a reputation for lawlessness. Though Ribbonism has been seen by many historians as a rather romantic form of self-defence adopted by a peasantry under assault from economic forces beyond their control, it is certain that Peel did not see them as anything other than a problem of law and order.

Peel's solution for Ireland was to create an Irish police force. In 1814 the so-called Peace Preservation Force was created. Peel had laid the basis for what would later become known as the Royal Irish Constabulary. This was a most significant achievement, paving the way for Peel's subsequent creation of the Metropolitan Police in London in 1829 and creating a blueprint for imperial police forces throughout the empire. Whether it worked in an Irish context is difficult to say. Unsurprisingly, the number of recorded crimes went up and, worryingly, a large percentage of the crimes seemed to involve clashes with the police. To some extent Peel had perhaps only exacerbated the problems.

The second immediate problem was the threat of famine, which reached acute levels in 1817. As Chief Secretary for Ireland, Peel responded pragmatically to the crisis caused by the partial failure of the potato crop, organising relief work and importing cheap maize.

Although Peel seems to have responded intelligently and humanely to problems in Ireland, his attitude to the sectarian question remained strongly Protestant. Indeed his hostility to Catholicism and the specific issue of Catholic civil rights was so strong that he had earned the nickname 'Orange Peel'. Furthermore, when Canning formed a liberal Tory administration in 1827 and promised to attempt an Emancipation bill, Peel ostentatiously resigned from the government. That Peel should, only one year later, have been one of the main voices to argue in favour of Emancipation is surely a measure of the impact of O'Connell's electoral victory at County Clare. But it is also a measure of the flexible and practical intelligence that made Peel such a skilful politician.

As we have seen, Peel shrewdly designed a bill which would both emancipate the Catholics and emasculate the Catholic Association by reducing the Irish electorate dramatically. This was, however, more than just a cunning manoeuvre. It was in many respects the beginning of a line of approach towards Ireland that influenced both Tory and Liberal political leaders until 1914. By giving concessions to Catholics, and in particular middling-class respectable Catholics, it was possible to positively demonstrate the advantages of being within the Union and simultaneously to remove the sense of grievance that tended to make Catholics become nationalists. In particular Peel sought to break what he called the 'powerful combination' between O'Connell and the Catholic hierarchy.

Ironically, of course, Catholic Emancipation also appeared to many on the so-called 'ultra' or right wing of the Tory Party to be a betrayal of the party's Protestant principles. Thus, in hindsight, we can see

Peel's neatly executed reverse-step over the Catholic issue as a step towards his own political demise. But this was of course not apparent in 1829 and the ensuing crisis over the Reform Act temporarily pushed Ireland out of the headlines and indeed pushed the Tories from power.

When Peel eventually returned as Prime Minister in 1841 he was not particularly interested in addressing Ireland. The Whigs in the previous eleven years had meddled continuously with Irish affairs and even allied themselves with O'Connell in the so-called Lichfield House Compact. As a result the Conservatives, including Peel, had reverted to their traditional Orange position.

By 1843, however, the Repeal movement was making a great deal of noise and the blusterings of Young Ireland, coupled with the endemic violence of Ribbonism, combined to encourage Peel to revive his earlier approach. In 1843 he established a commission under the Earl of Devon to investigate the issues surrounding the Land Question in Ireland. This was undoubtedly a sensible initiative. The emergence of tenant leagues in Ireland had threatened yet more disorder and highlighted the complaints of the poor peasantry. The commission was diligent and thorough. Unfortunately their recommendations came too late to avert the famine which in itself rendered any proposals rather irrelevant.

But Peel could not be expected to foresee the famine, and in 1844 he optimistically placed a whole range of reforming ideas for Ireland before his Cabinet. The overall aim was once again political: to detach moderate Catholics from the nationalist camp. In the event Peel's programme was defeated by an unholy combination of Protestant and Catholic prejudice, both in Westminster and in Ireland.

Peel proposed to address a number of major issues including franchise reform, landlord–tenant relations, Catholic education and rights to bequeath money to the church and above all the training of Catholic priests. The suggested £5 householder franchise fell at the first hurdle in the Commons. A bill to provide compensation for evicted tenants was defeated by the Lords. The Academic Colleges Act which established three university colleges which Catholics were entitled to attend – thereby removing their long-standing grievance that they could only acquire a high standard of education by going abroad – was destroyed in practice by the fact that both Catholics and Dissenting Protestants largely boycotted the institutions on the advice of their clergy. Their objection stemmed from the fact that Peel had stipulated that no theology would be taught in the colleges so as to avoid the explosive issues which might fuel sectarianism. This view was rather too logical for the men of God on both sides. In a rare outbreak of brotherly solidarity, they combined to denounce the colleges as 'godless'. Thus Peel's so-called Queen's Colleges almost entirely failed in their objective.

The Charitable Bequests Act of 1844, which legalised the gifting of private bequests to the Catholic Church by individuals, was marginally more successful though it too met rather disingenuous and ultimately ineffective opposition from the Catholic hierarchy, and indeed from O'Connell. But the most controversial policy was the so-called Maynooth Grant. The Maynooth Seminary was the main training college for priests throughout Ireland. It had been established by Pitt in the 1790s as a means of diminishing the connection between Ireland and Europe and had received a small grant at its inception. By 1845 the college was in financial difficulties, so Peel proposed to triple the grant and make the principle of governmental assistance a permanent one. Such an enlightened proposal, though obviously entirely consistent with Peel's political aims, caused a wave of indignation in Britain. The government was assailed by over 8,000 petitions from Protestant communities and the Tory Party once again revived the charge of betrayal against Peel. The bill did become law but Peel's party was badly split and it passed only because O'Connell and the radical Whigs chose to support it.

In conclusion it seems pretty clear that most of Peel's efforts in Ireland were not very successful. The best that can be argued for Peel is that he was most successful before and after he was actually Prime Minister. As Chief Secretary and Home Secretary he has a number of credits, most famously Catholic Emancipation itself. And after his fall he clearly left a very fertile legacy for subsequent Prime Ministers to draw upon. The most obvious inheritor of the Peelite approach to Ireland was, of course, Gladstone. Despite the fact that Gladstone would later go much further than Peel and even eventually adopt Home Rule, which was in many ways Repeal by another name, the fundamental belief that Anglo-Irish tensions could be solved with enlightened legislation was essentially Peelite. Die-hard Protestants and Tories might argue that such a dangerous legacy should not be seen as any sort of success. It is certainly true that Ireland became mixed up in the debates over free trade and repeal of the Corn Laws which split the Conservative Party and left it in the political 'wilderness' for twenty years. Appropriately enough Gladstone, inspired by Peel, later did just the same for the

Liberals: attempting Home Rule and instead splitting his party. Put like that, it does not seem such a successful legacy, but that is perhaps too harsh. The belief in a legislative solution is probably a better illusion than any of the bloodier 'solutions' proposed before and since.

It can be argued that Peel might be seen as the founder of the Conservative approach that later became known as 'Constructive Unionism', half-heartedly practised by Salisbury and Balfour, between 1886 and 1905. There is a little truth in this, but Constructive Unionism amounted to little in practice except land reform and, given that Peel managed no land reform, the argument seems a little thin.

In the last analysis, despite the legacy, it seems clear that Peel was not successful in dealing with Ireland. Most of his measures did not become law and those that did caused outrage, often among the people they were designed to help. Sectarian passions were inflamed, land issues were not dealt with and reform of higher education became a farce. In political terms, O'Connellite demands for self-government were silenced not by Peel but by the coming famine. They would resurface again in the 1870s and 1880s and dog British politics until the Great War. Peel not only failed to appease the majority of Irish men and women; he roused Protestant bigotries in England to such a pitch that Anglo-Irish relations were worse in 1846 than in 1841, and the famine was about to add a good deal more poison to the well. On top of that, Peel had split his own party, condemning it to opposition for a generation, and wrecked his own career. All this can only lead to one conclusion: that Peel's Irish policies as Prime Minister, though honourable and intelligent in aim, were, seen from any angle, quite impressively disastrous.

Questions

1. How accurate is it to see Peel's Irish policies as a coherent policy of Constructive Unionism?
2. How far can it be argued that Peel's Irish policies between 1841 and 1846 seriously damaged his career? (This question should also include some analysis of his actions during the famine. See Chapter 3.)

SOURCES

1. O'CONNELL'S AIMS AND METHODS

Source A: From a Report of the Committee of the Catholic Association (1824).

They [Irish Catholics] know that their cause is just and holy. It is the cause of religion and liberty. It is the cause of their country and their God. But, in order effectively to exert the energies of the Irish people, pecuniary resources are absolutely necessary . . . Your committee propose: that a monthly subscription should be raised throughout Ireland, to be denominated 'The Catholic Monthly Rent' . . . care to be taken to publish in or near each Catholic chapel as may be permitted by the clergy, the particulars of the sums subscribed and that the amount shall not exceed one penny per month.

Source B: Extract from O'Connell's electoral address reported in Freeman's Journal (26 June 1828).

The oath at present required by law [for MPs] is, 'That the sacrifice of the Mass and the Invocation of the blessed Virgin Mary and other saints, as now practised by the Church of Rome, are impious and idolatrous'. Of course, I will never stain my soul with such an oath; I leave that to my honourable opponent, Mr. Vesey Fitzgerald [the Conservative MP for Clare]. He has often taken that horrible oath; he is ready to take it again, and asks your votes to enable him so to swear. I would rather be torn limb from limb than take it.

Source C: From O'Connell's correspondence (February 1833).

My plan is to restore the Irish Parliament with the full assent of Protestants and Presbyterians as well as Catholics. I desire no social revolution, no social change. The nobility to possess lands, titles and legislative privileges as before the Union. The Clergy, for their lives, their full incomes – to decrease as Protestantism may allow that decrease. The landed Gentry to enjoy their present state, *being residents*.

Every man to be considered a resident who has an establishment in Ireland.

In short, salutary restoration without revolution; an Irish Parliament, British connection, one King, two legislatures.

Source D: From John Mitchel's gaol journal (Mitchel was a leading figure in the Young Ireland movement).

He [O'Connell] led them [the Irish people] as I believe all wrong for forty years. He was a lawyer, and could never come to the point of denying and defying British law. He was a Catholic, sincere and devout; and would not see that the Church had ever been the enemy of Irish freedom. He was an aristocrat by position and by taste; and the name of a Republic was odious to him.

Source E: From O'Connell's speech as his own defence counsel at his trial (January 1844).

From the day when first I entered the arena of politics until the present hour, I have never neglected an opportunity of impressing upon the minds of my fellow countrymen the fact, that I was an apostle of that political sect who held that liberty was only to be attained under such agencies as were strictly consistent with the law and the constitution – that freedom was to be attained, not by the effusion of human blood, but by the constitutional combination of good and wise men; by perseverance in the courses of tranquillity and good order, and by an abhorrence of violence and bloodshed. It is my proudest boast, that throughout a long and eventful life, I have faithfully devoted myself to the promulgation of that principle, and, without vanity, I can assert, that I am the first public man who ever proclaimed it.

Questions

1. What do Sources A and B reveal about the way Catholicism was being used by O'Connell and the Catholic Association in the 1820s? (4 marks)
2. Explain why Mitchel, in Source D, felt that O'Connell had led the Irish people 'all wrong' for forty years. (4 marks)
3. Does Source E prove that O'Connell was absolutely opposed to the use of violence as a means of furthering his political aims? (5 marks)
4. Use all the sources and your own knowledge to evaluate O'Connell's abilities as an Irish nationalist leader. (5 marks)
*5. What does Source C suggest about the nature of O'Connell's nationalism? (7 marks)

Worked answer

*5. O'Connell's letter of 1833 casts the great 'Liberator' in a curiously timid role. He is at great pains to declare that he is merely seeking 'restoration' (of Grattan's Parliament) and not 'revolution'. His would appear to be an Irish nationalism that could coexist with belief in the British monarchy and, of course, the British Empire. The formulaic slogan 'one King, two Parliaments' would not be acceptable to many nationalists that were to follow, such as Young Ireland, the Fenians and Sinn Féin.

At best one might suggest that O'Connell shows himself as some-one who defined his nationalism rather narrowly in terms of legal rights, and even here rejected the idea of any complete constitutional severance between the two islands.

On wider social issues such as the question of land ownership there is a fairly unambiguous commitment to the status quo, or the 'present state' as he termed it. Evidently as a man of the Irish gentry himself he was not about to pose as any kind of social radical. Even the rather gentle call for a reduction in the income of Protestant clergy – this being a reference to the fact that Catholics were still paying a tithe of sorts which helped to sustain a Protestant clergy – seems to be more of a respectful suggestion than a confident demand. Taken at face value, then, it is clear why more ardent and thoroughgoing nationalists, such as Mitchel in Source D, would have criticised O'Connell's approach as weak and uninspiring.

We must, however, be aware of the historical context in which this letter was written. In 1833 O'Connell was not in a strong position politically to push his Repeal movement. In order for it to have any chance of success he would have to gradually build support for the idea amongst all sorts of groups, and for this reason it is not surpris-ing that it is couched in such moderate terms. O'Connell was clearly trying very hard to woo Irish Protestants to his cause, which almost certainly explains the pledge of loyalty to the monarchy, the cautious approach to clerical pay and of course the clear signal that a restored Parliament would require the 'full assent' of all shades of religious opinion. In that light we can see him as skilfully distancing himself from the idea that he was a Catholic champion only. However, it has to be said that the failure of the Repeal campaign shows that he never quite achieved this. O'Connell's Irish nationalism was never one that Protestants could subscribe to easily.

Even his apparent caution on social questions might be seen in tactical terms. In order to make any headway politically he would need the help of the Protestant Ascendancy in Ireland, many of whom carried great influence within British political parties.

We must then be a little careful before declaring that O'Connell was a moderate or conservative nationalist. Although it seems likely that his belief in the value of the 'British connection' was genuine and his all-round caution did inevitably reflect the values of his class, it is also true he always allowed his nationalist beliefs to be circumscribed and shaped by the political context in which he operated. In that sense we can say that his was a cautious nationalism because it was, as he saw things, the nationalism of the possible.

SOURCES

2. THE ROLE OF RELIGION IN O'CONNELL'S POLITICAL CAMPAIGNS

Source F: A newspaper report of a march by the Catholic Association into the largely Protestant town of Ballybay in Ulster.

A conflict ensued immediately. How it commenced is not well known; but the termination was awfully fatal. One Catholic was run through the body with a sword or bayonet, and died on the spot. Another had his leg shattered by a musket ball, and is lying, with little hopes of recovery. Several, it is supposed, must have been slightly wounded, as they were fired upon for nearly a mile during their retreat.

Source G: From a speech by Revd Henry Cooke, the Presbyterian leader of Protestant opposition to O'Connell's Repeal movement. Speaking in Belfast, 1841.

Look at the town of Belfast. When I was myself a youth I remember it almost a village. But what a glorious sight does it now present – the masted grove within our harbour – (cheers) – our mighty warehouses teeming with the wealth of every climate – (cheers) – our giant manufactories lifting themselves on every side – (cheers) – our streets marching on. All this we owe to the Union. No, not all – for throned above our fair town, and looking serenely from our mountain's brow, I behold the genii of Protestantism and Liberty . . .

Source H: From O. MacDonagh's *O'Connell: The Life Of Daniel O'Connell, 1775–1847* (London: Weidenfeld & Nicolson, 1991).

For a nineteenth century Catholic, O'Connell was as remarkable for his commitment to the total separation of church and state as for his unqualified defence of the individual's liberty of conscience . . . He was a tireless advocate of the English dissenters' cause, from the abolition of religious tests for office to the abolition of church rates, and despite the chasms in creed, he remained on good terms with almost all, and in particular with the Society of Friends.

Source I: From R.F. Foster's *Modern Ireland, 1600–1972* (London: Penguin, 1988).

Wellington (who from 1825 had been looking for a conciliatory settlement to the Emancipation issue) described the Catholic clergy, nobility, lawyers and gentry as 'a sort of theocracy', governing Ireland with the backing of Rome. As he went on to point out, the exclusion of Catholics from formal power had not succeeded in restricting their *social* power – or, as it happened, their political *influence*. In 1829 their claims, made manifest, created a formal constitutional revolution . . . The manner of its passing [Catholic Emancipation] . . . gave a Catholic middle-class 'ascendancy' a vital psychological boost.

Source J: From Patrick O'Farrell's *England and Ireland since 1800* (London: Oxford University Press, 1975).

Having been forced to give ground on the Emancipation issue, English attitudes hardened against any further concessions to political Catholicism. O'Connell had erected an Irish nationalism on a sectarian base. The result was to link Irish nationalism with Catholicism into a most effective political force. But it was also to confirm the sectarian hostility of the time so profoundly as to nullify later attempts by Irish nationalists to bridge the sectarian chasm O'Connell's movement had opened up. In the long term, the cost of Catholic emancipation was to be partition.

Questions

1. How far does Source G explain why Ulster Protestants opposed the Repeal movement? (2 marks)
2. Use Source H and your own knowledge to discuss the view that, in political terms, O'Connell was more of a liberal than a Catholic. (3 marks)
*3. In what way does Source I throw new light on the position of Catholics in Ireland before Emancipation? (6 marks)

4. Use Source J and your own knowledge to discuss the view that the 'cost of Catholic emancipation was to be partition'. (6 marks)
5. Do the sources support the view that O'Connell did more to divide Ireland than unite it? (8 marks)

Worked answer

*3. There is something about Anglo-Irish history which induces in the English mind a tendency to think in clichés. One of the principal clichés is that Catholic Ireland consisted of nothing much more than hordes of semi-starving peasants who had been brutally oppressed from the time of Cromwell onwards, more or less continuously. In this caricatured past O'Connell appears as a uniquely charismatic shepherd driving the unthinking peasantry onward. Foster, however, hints at an entirely different reality.

O'Connell was not unique; he is better understood as only the most prominent of a class of Catholics who were far more powerful than the stereotype suggests. It is apparent that Ireland had a Catholic bourgeoisie which was in effect already governing Ireland as businessmen, as priests, as barristers and, most importantly, as what might be termed 'men of influence'. This is not to say that the Protestant Ascendancy was not powerful but simply to point out that the idea of a ruling class in Ireland is far more complex than is often thought. To some extent class lines cut across sectarian lines.

What is particularly interesting is that Wellington seems to have realised the need to 'buy off' what might be seen as a Catholic Ascendancy, well before Emancipation and indeed before Peel developed that analysis into a clear set of policies for his government of 1841. Peel's controversial reforms in Ireland, such as the Maynooth bill, can all be understood as an attempt to win the support of what Wellington rather exaggeratedly called the 'Catholic Theocracy'. Thus understood, English policy in Ireland can be seen in a similar way to Peel's policy in England: namely to embrace the new money in order to keep the old money in power.

In conclusion, it is clear that in many ways Wellington's view recasts traditional assumptions about Ireland almost entirely. Emancipation becomes not a hard-won victory for a downtrodden people but merely a recognition of the fact that many of that religion were now too powerful to ignore.

3

THE GREAT FAMINE AND ITS LEGACY, 1845–70

BACKGROUND NARRATIVE

Towards the end of the summer of 1845 the rain that fell far and wide across Ireland carried within it spores of a fungus that would soak down deep into the soil. This invisible invader was to bring death and devastation to more 'Britons' than would die in the Great War of 1914–18.

The causes of the Great Famine can be expressed in absurdly simple terms or bewilderingly complex ones. At its most straightforward there occurred what might be called a terrible accident. A strain of fungus, *Phytophthora infestans*, hitherto unknown in Ireland, entered the country from northern Europe. The fungus caused a savage potato blight which devastated a third of the crop of 1845, three-quarters of it in 1846, and then, after a respite in 1847, returned to severely deplete the crop of 1848. Thousands of people, particularly children and the old, literally starved to death, and diseases such as typhus and cholera swept through the poorer, weakened population. Unlike in the Great War, no detailed record of the fallen was kept, but it is approximated by historians that around a million died.

The blight was first noted in the British press in September 1845. Initially local churches, and the Quakers in particular, bore the burden of relief but as the problem became clear, the British Prime Minister, Robert Peel, took decisive steps to alleviate the suffering. In November 1845 he set up a Relief Commission to oversee the ₖ of helping the hungry and he also purchased £100,000 worth of indian maize from America to be used to feed the destitute. Nevertheless, he did not intend to give the corn away free: he created a Board of Works in January 1846 to provide road-building schemes to provide the poor with a means of making enough money to pay for the corn. He also hoped that the introduction of cheaper food into the market would help to keep the price of other foodstuffs down.

Peel's response would eventually prove to be seriously inadequate but it is certainly true that few died in 1845 or early 1846. However, it was Ireland's misfortune that the potato crisis became entangled with the political crisis at Westminster over the repeal of the Corn Laws. In June 1846 Peel was forced out of office as a result of his controversial repeal of the Corn Laws, an act in itself motivated partly by his desire to allow bread prices to fall in Ireland. This proved to be a deeply unfortunate turn of events for Ireland as the resultant Whig ministry, under Lord John Russell, was firmly committed to *laissez-faire* economic principles. Put simply, this economic philosophy states that governments should not interfere with market forces. In short, Russell believed that to give free food to Ireland would be to risk ruining those whose income depended upon selling food and, even worse, to encourage the peasantry to expect charity and therefore to take no steps to help themselves.

Since it was widely believed that such individual 'self-help' was the very reason for Britain's great wealth and progress and that the lack of such enterprise was the reason for Ireland's poverty, it became a fixed idea in Whig circles that Ireland must be made to learn from this disaster. Charity would only make matters worse in the long run. It would be difficult to overestimate the extent to which such ideological rigidity exacerbated the crisis in Ireland. Interestingly Peel also shared these views but was, despite his reputation for coldness, a little more prepared to make an exception in the circumstances.

As Russell's government came into office the price of good potatoes in Ireland was beginning to inflate far beyond anything the landless labourers or small peasant farmers could afford. At the start of 1845 the cheap 'Lumper' potato had been 16 pence a hundredweight; by the end of 1846 it was at 6 shillings (72 pence) a hundredweight. Though Russell maintained the Public Works schemes, it was fast becoming clear that the poorer classes could not expect to buy their salvation. It remains a disturbing fact that in 1846 more grain was being exported from Ireland than imported.

The winter of 1846–7 was particularly bad and the death rate rose sharply, particularly in the poor regions of Connacht and Munster. The only hope for many was to join the Public Works schemes. By March 1847 three-quarters of a million were building roads in freezing conditions. Horrifying reports of roadside deaths and bodies eaten by dogs began to circulate in the British press. Russell responded by passing the Destitute Poor Act which established soup kitchens for the starving. This was probably the most effective measure taken by the Russell ministry at any time during the crisis. By July 1847 the soup kitchens were providing three million meals a day.

The mood at Westminster was one of anger with the Irish landlords who, it was felt, had failed in their duties of both caring for their tenants and creating an efficient agricultural system in the first place. It was felt that the landlords were now simply 'howling' for English money to solve an Irish problem. The fact that the British government had justified the Act of Union precisely because it would make Ireland a part of the United Kingdom seemed strangely forgotten. In response to this mood Russell passed the notorious Poor Law Extension Act in June 1847 which transferred the cost of 'outdoor relief' to the Irish rates. In other words, Russell insisted that the Irish should solve their own problem.

In 1848 the blight returned with devastating impact upon a very weak people. The situation was made worse by the fact that Russell had closed down the soup kitchens in September 1847 and ordered the Relief Commissioners home, assuming the famine to be over. The impression was of a government that had simply washed its hands of the Irish people.

Desperate landlords, now faced with the cost of relief, escalated the trend to evict starving people from their smallholdings, thereby moving the problem and simultaneously consolidating their estates. The number of evictions throughout the famine was astonishingly high, though it must be added that a minority of landlords risked their own bankruptcy by seeking ways to feed and support their tenants. Given that tenants had long since stopped paying rent and that the British government expected the landlords to meet the cost of famine relief, it is perhaps not surprising that many in turn resorted to callous measures.

By 1848 the response of the peasantry to their suffering had become one of passive resignation. There was a farcical uprising led by the Young Ireland movement but the lack of support for it illuminates the stupefied and stunned mood in Ireland more than it expresses the lack of nationalist sentiment. By 1850 the worst was over, but the legacy and significance still remain a matter of historiographical controversy.

ANALYSIS (1): HOW FAR, IF AT ALL, SHOULD THE BRITISH GOVERNMENT BE BLAMED FOR TRAGIC CONSEQUENCES OF THE POTATO BLIGHT IN IRELAND?

This is a very dangerous question. It is a question which is more likely to explode into a mess of prejudices than it is to provide a clear answer. But the problem remains that for Irish nationalists it was, as the Young Ireland nationalist John Mitchel said, 'God who sent the blight but the English who made the famine'.[1] It is an assertion that demands attention. Obviously it is also a belief that nurtures a militant, even violent, nationalism and, as such, the answer to the question becomes decidedly loaded with consequence.

What might be called the darker green nationalist view consists of a number of interlocking beliefs. Firstly, it is assumed that the conditions that made Ireland so vulnerable – widespread poverty, over-dependence on one crop and a population that was growing at a dangerously fast rate – were all manifestations of an underdevelopment that was the consequence of being too close to England at the time of the Industrial Revolution. The latter process pulled labour and capital from Ireland into the industrial centres of England. Thus it can be argued that Ireland's poverty and relative backwardness were in part by-products of English advancement: as if Ireland were little more than an exploited colony. It can also be argued that too many of the wealthy in Ireland were in fact part of the alien Protestant class who had deprived the Irish of their land and then proved far too Anglophile to support Ireland's claims.

The most powerful allegations against England, however, are concerned not so much with the preconditions of famine as with the way the government responded after the initial crop failures. At its simplest this can be a tale with one particular villain: Charles

Trevelyan, the Assistant Secretary to the Treasury and the man responsible for directing famine relief. It was Trevelyan who seemed to believe that it was more important to sustain the sacred principle of *laissez-faire* economics than it was to save lives. Of course, Trevelyan can also be seen as the embodiment of English attitudes. And there is truth in such a view.

It was Ireland's misfortune that the famine occurred at a time when the doctrine of *laissez-faire* or free trade economics had become an unquestioned orthodoxy amongst the majority of ministers and civil servants. Ironically, perhaps, it was Peel, the Tory Prime Minister, who is often seen as being more humane in his response to the famine than the Whig Russell, who established the triumph of free trade with the repeal of the Corn Laws in 1846. Arguably Peel's handling of the crisis would have been little better than Russell's if he had stayed in power. It is certainly true that the ruling elites of both parties had convinced themselves that matters of trade, of supply and demand of any particular good, were not a proper area for government intervention and that such matters should be left to what Trevelyan called 'natural causes'. In other words, the markets were deemed to be self-regulating mechanisms, in which problems would eventually resolve themselves. Any attempt to interfere – for example, by supplying free food to a starving people – would have disastrous consequences for other food producers who were being so dramatically undercut. Worse still, the poor peasantry, in receiving free food, would find no incentive to work hard for higher wages or to reorganise the nature of their agricultural business so that this would not happen again. Thus it became possible to believe in England that non-intervention was the only way that the Irish would learn a valuable lesson. Cruelty was in fact kindness.

These attitudes were reinforced by a number of other widespread assumptions. The political economist Thomas Robert Malthus had argued years before that any famine was in some respects only nature's way of correcting overpopulation. He was not referring directly to Ireland but when the famine struck it was easy for educated men to see the tragedy as merely a painful but inevitable Malthusian adjustment to the mismatch between productive capacity and population. Hence Malthusian views dovetailed rather neatly with free trade views, producing a conviction that not much either could or should be done.

But the nationalist case would suggest that all these fine logical and theoretical assumptions grew from the soil of something uglier and altogether more irrational: a racist contempt for the Irish that was so potent that it was prepared to countenance something close to what extreme nationalists have called genocide.

There can be little doubt that there was a widespread feeling at Westminster that the Irish had to some extent brought this on themselves. *The Times* for example spoke of John Bull's resentment at having to 'pay for the delinquencies of others'. Like many other influential commentators, *The Times* believed that the root problem lay in the character of Irishmen. When Disraeli, the future Tory Prime Minister, wrote in 1836 that the Irish were a 'wild reckless, indolent, uncertain and superstitious race',[2] his comments would not have raised an eyebrow in the gentlemen's clubs of London. The respected Victorian historian J.A. Froude described the Irish as being 'more like squalid apes than human beings'.[3] Such attitudes are scattered throughout the letters of Victorian England. The English stereotype of the Irish was of a race that was predisposed to be indolent (the potato being the lazy man's crop), superstitious, though this is often a Protestant term for 'Catholic', drunken, garrulous, ungrateful, improvident and, by bewildering turns, childishly sentimental and ferociously violent. With this arsenal of adjectives it was possible to explain away the famine as a punishment for improper behaviour: perhaps even as a divine punishment. Or as Trevelyan put it, assuming the famine to have been a lesson sent from on high, 'Supreme Wisdom has educed permanent good out of transient evil'.[4] Oddly, the idea of a divine punishment chimed in with the fatalistic logic of the starving poor themselves.

Such a powerful cocktail of negative attitudes, coupled with free trade ideas and Malthusian complacency, underpinned the government's response to the crisis. The government's set of responses – the initial import of cheap grain, the Public Works schemes, the soup kitchens and the eventual attempt to force the whole problem on to the Irish Poor Law system – was undoubtedly pitifully inadequate. And it seems that some of that inadequacy was not just the result of inflexible attachment to theories but in some degree the result of an indifference born of a racial contempt. That is not to say that John Mitchel was right, but rather that there is some truth in explanations which centre on England's brutal complacency.

But historians who are prepared to trade in the dangerous currency of blame must then also be prepared to look at the way certain sections of Irish society gained at the expense of others, in other words to go beyond the simple dichotomy between evil English and downtrodden Irish in order to see that in fact the tensions between the suffering and the indifferent were as much within Ireland itself.

One can identify perhaps the most famous example of Irish exploitation of the Irish in the controversial Gregory clause – the amendment of the Poor Law Act by the Irish MP for Dublin, William Gregory, which stipulated that any family owning more than a quarter of an acre must give up their land before being entitled to claim relief. The Gregory clause was in effect a charter for land clearance: the prime means by which the structure of land ownership was changed in Ireland. There can be no doubt that the famine did alter the pattern of land ownership, even possibly for the better, but in that fact there is concealed another: many Irishmen actually gained and prospered as a result of the suffering of their fellow Irishmen. It would be absurd to seek to explain this by simply laying the blame on an Anglo-Irish landlord class. The Gregory family and their kind were as Irish as the Wolfe Tones or the Parnells, indeed Gregory's wife went on to lead the Gaelic literary revival later in the century. More importantly, we must admit that Irish society was a complex and graded one. The famine affected different groups in different ways. For the poorer landless labourers and the cottier class, the famine was an unmitigated disaster. But surely for many commercial traders and more middling-class Irishmen, the inflation in food prices must have been a time of increased profit. The famine created all manner of winners and losers and it is exceptionally difficult to talk of blame in such situations, but it seems that in many respects the complacency of the English was abetted and aided by the greed and business sense of sections of the Irish. To put it another way, the famine has to be understood in vertical class terms as well as in racial or national terms. It must also be added that the famine varied considerably by region. It would be possible to build an argument that the commercial centres in the east, such as Dublin and Belfast, gained at the expense of the west. Without pursuing this idea, it should be clear that the famine has to be understood as something impacting upon a complex society, with all manner of varied effects, each of which was exacerbated or ameliorated by other factors, either within or without Ireland itself. Once we begin to allow that complexity, the simple division of the history into victims and villains begins to sound rather crude.

Indeed, recent trends in the historiography of the famine, by Irish so-called revisionist historians at least, have tended to avoid the language of blame altogether. The tone has been cool and dispassionate. Perhaps the leading authority on the famine in the last two decades has been Cormac Ó Gráda and he has treated the famine as something of such multi-factoral complexity that the notion of finding any one group to blame is quickly reduced to an irrelevance. Instead we have a famine which in Ó Gráda's words is best understood as 'a tragic ecological accident'.[5] Nothing as potent as *Phytophthora infestans* had been seen before. The timing of the arrival of this fungus was about as bad as it could have been. Had it arrived earlier or later, the damage would not have been so great. Instead it arrived when all the factors that would dramatically magnify its impact were in place. Before the 1840s dependence on the potato and indeed population growth were both less marked. After mid-century the capacity of countries such as America to export food cheaply had improved dramatically and even in England politicians such as Gladstone had reversed the idea that Ireland was best left alone. There is, then, a good case for saying that the blight struck at the worst possible of times and that no blame can be attached to such random acts of nature.

The truth about the famine is uniquely difficult to grasp. Partly this is due to the complexity of the subject, the number of interacting causal and exacerbating elements being so great, but partly also because it is so difficult to find an appropriate language for such horror. The dispassionate revisionists are as likely to seem insensitive to human suffering as the nationalist Anglophobes are to seem crude hijackers of the past. That said, it does seem to be true that the government in England should share some part of the blame for the way in which it amplified the scale of the suffering. But just how much that point should be stressed would seem to depend upon the distorting demands of prejudice and political correctness.

Questions

1. Explain why the British authorities felt justified in offering Ireland relatively little aid during the famine crisis.
2. The Great Famine was a tragic accident. Discuss.

ANALYSIS (2): TO WHAT EXTENT DID THE GREAT FAMINE CHANGE THE NATURE OF THE IRISH QUESTION?

There can be little doubt that the Great Famine marks a major turning point in Irish history. Measuring the consequences in the simplest and bleakest of ways, it can be said that the Great Famine led directly to the deaths of approximately one million people and by 1850 to the emigration of a further one and a half million. Obviously this is a tragedy or, to be a little more precise, an almost unimaginable collection of individual and familial tragedies. But this kind of significance is largely cut off from the historian as so few of the dead left records of their suffering and as even accurate records of the names and numbers of the dead were not kept. When we compare that with the meticulous way in which, for example, the Imperial War Graves Commission carved the name of each and every one of the 'fallen' in the Great War, it is hard to resist the view that somehow the Great Famine has not been awarded great significance either by modern Britain or indeed by a modernising Ireland, both preferring to look ahead rather than back.

However, on a more prosaic level, it is certainly possible to see the famine as ushering in some very important socio-economic changes. There can be no doubt that it accelerated dramatically a painful and, as it turned out, prolonged reversal of demographic trends in Ireland. In the fifty years before the famine the Irish population had been growing at an extraordinary rate, reaching eight million by 1841. By 1851 that figure had fallen to six million and by the end of the century it had tumbled to around four million. To set this in context, Ireland was the only country in Western Europe to see its population decline in the second half of the nineteenth century. Obviously not all of this decline can be attributed to the Great Famine and there were signs of a slowing in the growth rate even before the blight, but it looks as though we can ascribe the primary cause to the famine.

Of course such a sharp decline has all sorts of knock-on consequences. The shortages of labour place a considerable restriction on economic growth and it might well be argued that Ireland's relative economic backwardness was also, in part, the by-product of this demographic shift. By contrast, Britain's successful transition to an industrial economy was made possible by the quadrupling of the nation's population in the nineteenth century.

The demographic revolution necessarily redrew the patterns of landholding in Ireland. To put it in broad terms, it appears that the general dislocation caused by the famine had serious consequences for those at either end of the rural social spectrum. The very poor such as the landless labourers and the cottier class were devastated. Although there were obviously regional variations, in the more barren parts of Ireland the whole class of poor and small landholders were erased from the landscape. This in turn allowed the wealthier tenant farmer to buy up land and consolidate his estate. Before the famine less than a third of farms were over 15 acres; by 1851, just over a half were of that size. At the same time, one farm in four had been wiped out.

At the other end of the scale, the crisis also hit the landlord class hard. The famine had increased the demand on their poor rates and yet frequently reduced the number of people paying rents on their land. This led to quite a few bankruptcies, which in turn often led to the quick sale of land. Overall then, it would be crudely true to say that the famine actually helped to create a larger class of middle-ranking tenant farmers, a group who would become politically crucial over the subsequent generation.

The nature of agricultural production also changed. By 1876 the acreage devoted to grain and potatoes was half that of the figure on the eve of the famine. The Irish farmer was switching to livestock farming. But perhaps one of the cruellest paradoxes of the famine is the fact that it ultimately improved the living standards of the Irish farmer and agricultural worker. The relative shortage of labour drove wage rates up and the plummeting population allowed those who remained behind to enjoy a healthy food supply. The Great Famine would prove to be the last famine in Ireland.

It has also been argued that the famine imprinted the Irish mentality with a tendency to look for escape or advancement through emigration. Although emigration was common even before the Great Famine, the impact of the 1840s affected the outlook of several generations to come. It is no exaggeration to say that the famine was the catalysing event in an Irish exodus so profound that by 1890 three million men and women of Irish birth lived abroad. To put it another way, at the end of the nineteenth century, 39 per cent of the entire population of Irish-born people no longer lived in Ireland. Given that many of those born of Irish parents abroad would also count themselves as Irish, it is not surprising that historians talk of an Irish empire. In particular the American Irish would decisively help to shift the nature of the Irish question by providing funds and armaments for subsequent generations of nationalists, particularly the Fenians.

Perhaps surprisingly, the famine did not immediately precipitate a major political reaction from Irish nationalists. Though it is a commonplace of history textbooks that hunger leads to revolt – one thinks for example of the key role of bread protests in both the French and Russian Revolutions – in Ireland it seems that the hunger so weakened the population that the will to rebel barely existed.

However, it would be wrong to say that Ireland was entirely quiescent. The year 1848 is known as the year of revolutions in European history, rebellion spreading from Paris through almost all of Europe's major cities like a bush fire. Even in London a huge gathering of Chartists, led by the flame-haired Irishman Feargus O'Connor, threatened the regime to such an extent that the Queen was sent to the Isle of Wight and 85,000 special constables enrolled. But Ireland's 1848 was rather closer to farce than high drama. A small rebellion led by members of the Young Ireland movement culminated in the battle of Widow McCormack's cabbage patch in Ballingarry near Tipperary. When two of the rebels were killed the movement collapsed and the leaders were captured and sentenced to transportation. In short, the rising was truly pathetic. But it would be wrong to think that the political consequences of the famine fizzled out in a cabbage patch.

Inevitably the way that the famine altered the social structure of Ireland was reflected in a new type of politics centred upon the demands of the tenant farmer. The 1850s saw the emergence of numerous tenant leagues and eventually a national Land League was created which became a vital driving force in the emergence of a new, powerful nationalist movement behind the imperious Parnell. More pertinent perhaps, the Land League played an important part in defending and improving the rights of the tenant farmers during the great agricultural depression which began in 1879. In some curious way the fatalism and political weakness of the Irish peasantry in the 1840s gave rise to a determination never to be in such a position again. In that way, perhaps, the folk memory of the famine inspired the next generation to turn the land question into one of the central questions of the day. So successful was the League in doing this that both British parties gave considerable concessions. Gladstone's 1881 Land Act and the Tory Wyndham Act of 1903 can be seen as the twin triumphs of the Land movement in Ireland, as a result of which the tenant farmers were gradually turned into owner-occupiers of their land. Indeed it could be argued, looking at the broad sweep of Irish history from the 1840s to the Great War, that the famine, for all its horrors, provided a psychological dynamic for a future social revolution in the countryside.

It might also reasonably be argued that the famine created a reservoir of anti-English feeling which nourished all manner of nationalist movements, but in particular the Fenians. It was John Mitchel of the Young Ireland movement who did more than anyone else to promote the view that the English conspired to deliberately let the Irish starve. Whatever the rights and wrongs of that view, it gained a currency particularly amongst emigrant communities, many of whom could trace their departure back to the Great Hunger. Again the Fenians, being first established in America, are perhaps the best example of the way in which folk memory of the famine translated into political action.

However, it would be wrong to say that Anglophobia swept through Ireland in the years after the tragedy. Indeed, it is remarkable how little anger and resentment seem to surface in Irish literature and journalism of the 1850s and 1860s. Indeed, Mitchel's view was very far from that of the typical Irish man or woman. In 1849 Queen Victoria visited Ireland and was welcomed with immense enthusiasm everywhere she went, a fact which suggests that the survivors did not harbour bitter resentment and furthermore that they did not see their calamity in political terms at all.

In Ireland itself the predominant view about the famine was one of despairing acceptance of a misfortune sent not by the English but by the Lord. For many, the potato blight was best understood as a divine punishment. Thus one of the most significant impacts of the famine was an increase in religiosity amongst the population. The 1850s saw what has been described as a 'devotional revolution' as the percentages of people attending mass rose to almost three times the pre-famine figure. It has also been calculated that the ratio of priests to lay-people dramatically increased, and it seems reasonable to assume that this also promoted a greater spirituality amongst the flock. This line of argument also touches upon a theory that the famine was responsible for destroying, or at least Christianising, a peasant culture which was to some extent semi-pagan in its reliance upon magic charms, rituals and incantations. Though there is some truth in this view, in that it was the poorer and less literate peasants who were the hardest hit, it is probably more accurate to suggest that the famine only accelerated what might be called the modernisation of Irish society. In the same way the famine only hastened the existing decline of the Gaelic language.

The famine changed the nature of Anglo-Irish relations largely because it utterly changed Ireland. In consequence the political agenda changed and new issues such as tenant rights began to assert themselves. More broadly, it served to sharpen the contrasts between the countries either side of the Irish Sea. Where England was urban, industrial and increasingly secular in outlook, Ireland was thrust back into rurality, industrial stagnation and a strict Catholicism. In conjunction with these fairly quantifiable effects there exists also an impact which is almost impossible to delineate: the way in which the horrors of the Great Hunger left a legacy of bitterness in the folk memory of the Irish people and amongst the Irish diaspora. If a united nation requires a shared historical experience to build its sense of identity, it seems reasonable to assume that the way the Union failed to treat the problem as a 'British' one must, in the longer term, have profoundly damaged the very idea of Union.

Questions

1. In what ways did the Great Famine change the nature of Irish society?
2. What were the political consequences of the Great Famine?
3. Charles Trevelyan has deservedly been portrayed as the embodiment of British callousness. How fair is this assessment?

SOURCES

1. CONTEMPORARY VIEWS OF THE FAMINE

Source A: Lord Clarendon, the Lord Lieutenant, to the Prime Minister, Lord John Russell (August 1847).

We shall be equally blamed for keeping the Irish alive or letting them die and we have only to select between the censure of the Economists or the Philanthropists – which do you prefer?

Source B: Extract from the Irish newspaper, the *Carlow Sentinel* (11 January 1847).

In these times for they are times of peril – men must speak out; and we shall do our duty fearlessly in calling on the non-residential proprietors to come forward and to lend their co-operation, or they will, when too late, regret the consequences of their neglect. In the Ballickmoyler district, Queen's County, a few, it is true, have contributed; but where are the names of the Earl

Kenmore, or of the Earl of Portarlington, upon whose estates a vast mass of hideous poverty exists? We have not yet heard that one shilling of their money has been contributed, although their agents draw large sums from the extensive estates.

Source C: A letter to the *Galway Mercury* from a Catholic clergyman, the Revd Mr Newel (8 March 1847).

I fear much that the want of coffins for the burial of the dead will cause them to be unburied, and to generate infection, more disastrous to human life than the want of food itself. The unusual occurrence here of a human being having been interred without the decency of a coffin took place in the parish of Ballinacourty a few days ago, when the corpse, after five or six days unburied, was at last sacked up in a coarse canvas and deposited in its parent earth. Another horrifying circumstance occurred near Oranmore, of a poor wretched woman named Redington, perishing during the night time, and in the morning her lifeless body was found partly devoured by rats.

Source D: A letter from Charles Trevelyan, Permanent Head of the Treasury (September 1848).

The poorest and most ignorant Irish peasant must, I think, by this time, have become sensible of the advantage of belonging to a powerful community like that of the United Kingdom, the establishments and pecuniary resources of which are at all times ready to be employed for his benefit. At any rate, the repeal of the Union will not be seriously demanded while so large a proportion of the Irish people are receiving Union wages and eating Union meal.

Source E: Editorial from *The Times* (22 September 1846).

Why was it that the prospect of, the certainty of a great calamity, did not animate [the Irish] to great exertions? Alas, the Irish peasant had tasted of famine and found that it was good. He saw the cloud looming in the distance and he hailed its approach. To him it teemed with goodly manna and salient waters.[6] He wrapped himself up in the mantle of inert expediency and said that he trusted to Providence. But the deity of his faith was the Government – the manna of his hopes was a Parliamentary grant.

Questions

*1. In what way do Sources B, C and E suggest very different underlying causes of the tragedy? (6 marks)

2. Do Sources A, D and E prove that the English authorities held a complacent and callous view of the problem? (5 marks)
3. How sound is Trevelyan's judgement about the strength of the Union in Source D? (5 marks)
4. How useful is Source C as evidence about the experiences of the Irish people during the famine? (4 marks)

Worked answer

*1. The three sources show something of the enormous complexity of this tragedy. Viewed from the comfort of *The Times* editorial office, it was easy to explain the crisis in racial terms. *The Times* appeared to believe that the Irish welcomed the famine as an opportunity to sponge off the English taxpayer. Their suffering was a 'mantle' or cloak to hide their feckless designs. When we set this breathtaking and racist arrogance against the image of rat-gnawed corpses it becomes evident that there were competing notions existing about the realities in Ireland even at the time. We should also note of course that this editorial was written relatively early in the crisis.

The *Carlow Sentinel* approached the problem from another popular perspective and in a sense highlighted another possible villain: the 'non-residential proprietor', more frequently referred to as the absentee landlord. There is much in the literature on this topic which suggests that the landlords did not do as much as they might have but this question is complicated by the fact that the response varied considerably from the indifferent to the humane. Indeed some landlords drove themselves to the brink of bankruptcy in their efforts to aid their tenantry and labourers. The source speaks of the immense wealth of the landlords but this was often not the case. In many ways the tragedy of the situation was that the landlords were expected, as some of the principal ratepayers, to find the money to fund the local government's aid schemes but lacked the capital to create such a sudden welfare system.

Perhaps the best that can be said of these limited sources is that they illuminate the fact that this famine, like most great panics, existed on a number of levels. At the level of popular journalism there swirled around the event an increasingly irrational cluster of scapegoat and/or conspiracy theories, whilst in the mundane world of human existence it was the small hard facts, such as the inability of the poor to provide coffins, which really mattered.

SOURCES

2. THE HISTORIOGRAPHICAL DEBATE

Source F: From *The Great Hunger* by Cecil Woodham-Smith (1962).

In the long and troubled history of England and Ireland no issue has provoked so much anger or so embittered relations between the two countries as the indisputable fact that huge quantities of food were exported from Ireland to England throughout the period when the people of Ireland were dying of starvation. 'During all the famine years,' wrote John Mitchel, the Irish revolutionary, 'Ireland was actually producing sufficient food, wool and flax to feed and clothe not nine but eighteen millions of people'; yet, he asserted, a ship sailing into an Irish port during the famine years with a cargo of grain was 'sure to meet six ships sailing out with a similar cargo'.

Source G: From *The Irish Famine* by Colm Tóibín and Diarmaid Ferriter (London: Profile Books, 1999).

Catholic society in Ireland in the 1840s was graded and complex, and to suggest that it was merely England or Irish landlords who stood by while Ireland starved is to miss the point. An entire class of Irish Catholics survived the Famine; many, indeed, improved their prospects as a result of it, and this legacy may be more difficult for us to deal with in Ireland now than the legacy of those who died or emigrated.

Source H: From *The Great Irish Famine* by Cormac Ó Gráda (Dublin: Gill & Macmillan, 1989).

In sum the Great Famine of the 1840s, instead of being inevitable and inherent in the potato economy, was a tragic ecological accident. Ireland's experience during these years supports neither the complacency exemplified by the Whig view of political economy nor the genocide theories espoused by a few nationalist historians.

Source I: From *The Great Irish Famine* by C. Póirtéir (Cork: Mercier Press, 1995).

The Landlords were not always to be blamed when evictions took place. Middlemen and well to do farmers were often responsible. 'Grabbing' was quite common: farmers who had money to spare were only too ready to approach the Landlord or his agent and offer to pay back rent on a neighbouring farm on the condition that they would be given possession.

Source J: From *England and Ireland since 1800* by P. O'Farrell (London and New York: Oxford University Press, 1975).

The Irish image was, from the 1840s, both dominated and epitomized by the famine, a catastrophe that did enormous and, it could be argued, ultimately fatal damage to the Union relationship. It provided Irish nationalists with material for a most fundamental indictment of England – the charge that it contrived the extermination and banishment of the Irish on the scale of mass murder.

Questions

1. Explain why O'Farrell, in Source J, argues that the famine damaged the Union. (4 marks)
*2. Explain why the points being made in Sources G and I might be thought to support a revisionist view of the famine. (7 marks)
3. In what ways do Sources F and G approach the issues differently? (7 marks)
4. How might it be argued that Ó Gráda (Source H) removes the idea of blame from the debate? (7 marks)

Worked answer

*2. Lurking within this question is an assumption that revisionism is a clear and easily identifiable approach. But is there really such a thing as a revisionist approach to Irish history? Whole books exist just to explore this question and happily discuss the position of such factions as the 'post-revisionists'. But it is probably best to avoid such sterile debates. To attempt a more common-sense definition: it may be said the revisionists sought to rescue Irish history from abuse at the hands of groups seeking to use history just as a source of propaganda. In that sense revisionism was about the deliberate demythologising of the past so that it no longer served simply to provide intellectual ammunition for the IRA or any other interested political grouping.

That said, both of these sources might be thought to be supportive of a revisionist view in the simple sense that they are at pains to detonate the old nationalist view that the blame for the deaths of around a million people should be laid at the feet of the English and/or unscrupulous landlords.

Tóibín begins the demolition by pointing out a fact which is unpalatable to many of the fiercer nationalists: that many Irish farmers exploited the disaster and actually improved their commercial position. Poirtier spells this out by pointing the finger at what are called the 'middlemen': men with enough capital to pay off overdue rents on the understanding that they would then take possession of the land. These Irish entrepreneurs would then force their fellow Irishmen off the land. Of course this is a very emotive assertion. Tóibín in particular is aware that to start reversing Mitchel's logic and begin picturing ordinary Irish farmers as somehow accomplices in what Mitchel called genocide would be, as Tóibín says, 'difficult for us to deal with'.

Implicit in Tóibín's last point is perhaps one of the key points of the revisionist agenda (if something as preconceived as that can be said to exist): the idea that Irish history must be looked at dispassionately. In that sense these sources perhaps do not present the revisionist standpoint very fairly. The point in the end is *not* to apportion blame but to break free from that sort of mind-set. But, perhaps oddly, by pointing out that the 'guilty' men were as often Irish as English, it may become possible to stop trading in such notions altogether.

4

THE AGE OF
PARNELL, 1870–90

BACKGROUND NARRATIVE

After the Great Famine and the collapse of the Repeal and Young Ireland movements, there was a short period in which British politicians in London could resort to their favourite Irish policy: masterly inactivity. But the government was to be jolted out of its imperial complacency by the violent actions of a new breed of Irish nationalists: the Fenians.

The Fenian Brotherhood was a secret society, dedicated to the overthrow of British rule in Ireland. It was first formed in America by veterans of the civil war but soon established a branch in Ireland itself. The organisation, though prone to internal quarrelling, proved to be one of the most enduring nationalist societies in history. Though the Fenians did not come close to their aim of over-throwing the British, there can be no doubt that in the 1860s the Fenians catalysed a new phase in Anglo-Irish relations.

The society first announced its political presence in 1866, with an absurd and utterly doomed attempt at invading and liberating Canada. Undaunted, in the spring of 1867 the Fenians attempted a nationalist revolution in Ireland, centred upon Dublin. However, due to shambolic organisation and infiltration by pro-British spies, the rising failed. Later in the same year the Fenians attempted a daring rescue of one of their imprisoned leaders, a Captain Kelly, by holding up a prison van in Manchester. Unfortunately, although Kelly was rescued, a policeman travelling in the van was shot dead in the process. Eventually the British authorities arrested, tried and convicted five Irishmen, four of whom were Fenians but none of whom had fired the shot which killed the policeman. Three of the men were hanged. Many felt the hanged men were not guilty of murder and nationalists spoke passionately about the 'Manchester Martyrs'. In December 1867 the Fenians attempted another high-risk rescue by blasting the walls of Clerkenwell prison in London. This time, due to an excessive use of explosive by the Fenians, a number of nearby houses were severely damaged and several civilians were killed.

This series of disturbances prompted the new leader of the Liberal Party, William Gladstone, to declare in 1868 that it was his 'mission to pacify Ireland'. In power, Gladstone adopted an approach that was clearly inspired by Peel's approach a generation earlier: to win Irish support for the Union by offering concessions and addressing existing Irish grievances, in effect to kill Fenianism with kindness. His first major concession was the Irish Church Act of 1869 which disestablished the Church of Ireland (i.e. the Anglican Church in Ireland), thereby removing a long-standing Catholic grievance that they were paying to maintain an alien church. Although this was fairly well received in Ireland, the most important issue there over the next generation would be the so-called Land Question. In bare outline the Land Question concerned the fraught relationship between landlords and tenants. The tenants had for many years complained about excessively high rents, absentee landlords and unwarranted evictions. There was also the deeper question about whether tenants who had farmed land for generations had any rights at law. Gladstone felt that this was an area in which enlightened legislation might help to bring stability.

In 1870 Gladstone passed his first Land Act which sought to give legal backing to the tenant farmers' notion of customary or traditional tenant rights, such as the right to compensation in the event of evictions or in the event of a departing tenant having made improvements to the land. Although this was a positive step, it fell a long way short of the demands of the various local tenant leagues that had been developing in parts of Ireland since the 1850s. In addition to this, the impact of the Great Agricultural Depression in the mid-1870s exacerbated tensions on the land. Inevitably the fall in agricultural prices put pressure on landlords to amalgamate holdings or switch to pasture. Also the rate of evictions and rent levels went up markedly. The tensions on the land increased gradually throughout the 1870s until in 1879 a so-called 'Land War' began.

The Land War was always something more than a mere struggle for tenant rights. In 1879 an Irish National Land League was set up under the presidency of a man who was to dominate Irish nationalist politics for over a decade: Charles Stewart Parnell.

Parnell was an unlikely leader of the tenantry and an unlikely leader of Irish nationalists in general, being a Protestant landlord with impressive credentials as a man of the Ascendancy elite. But Parnell had inherited his American mother's dislike of the English and saw himself very much in the mould of the Ascendancy patriots, such as Henry Grattan, who had won what was rather grandly termed 'legislative independence' for the Irish Parliament in 1782. It was Parnell's long-term aim to restore the Parliament which had closed with the Act of Union in 1800.

Parnell's real strength lay in the fact that he was not just president of the Land League; he was also an MP at Westminster and a respected figure amongst Fenians in America. He was, in short, able to hold a variety of the divergent strands of Irish nationalism together in a loose coalition that was dubbed the 'New Departure'. Gladstone was aware that Parnell was a powerful adversary and sought to compromise with him.

The Land War involved relatively little violence against the person. The strongest tactic developed by the Land League was the now famous 'Boycott' method in which the organised tenants would refuse to cooperate in any way or even speak to a landlord who was deemed to have acted unjustly. Parnell was himself imprisoned for inciting disorders. But eventually the struggle was largely resolved when Gladstone pushed through the important Land Act of 1881. This second Land Act was a major concession in that it gave the tenants what they had been long calling for, the so-called 3Fs: rights to a Fair Rent, Fixity of Tenure and a right of Free Sale of their tenure. But even after this, a significant obstacle remained. During the campaigns of the Land League Parnell had urged tenants involved in a conflict with their landlords simply to stop paying any rent. As the Land War came to a close the landlords insisted that their rent arrears be paid, but many tenants simply could not pay, hence an awkward impasse threatened to undermine the success of the second Land Act. It was perhaps Parnell's greatest coup that from prison he was able, through various intermediaries, to persuade Gladstone to pass another act, the Arrears Act of 1882, by which the government agreed to pay off most of the rent arrears. Although there was no written agreement between the two men it has become known as the 'Kilmainham Treaty', taking its name from the prison in which Parnell was held. Though this was a high price for the British government, they had in effect purchased an end to the Land War.

The brutal hacking to death of Gladstone's new Irish Chief Secretary, Lord Frederick Cavendish, and his Under-Secretary, T.H. Burke, in Phoenix Park only days after the 'treaty', perpetrated by a Fenian splinter group called the Invincibles – though a profound shock and a major political embarrassment to both Gladstone and Parnell – did not seem to destroy their new-found, if unofficial, working alliance.

With the partial victory in the Land War behind him, Parnell shifted his aim to the restoration of an Irish Parliament, a policy usually referred to as Home Rule. Initially Gladstone had been opposed to this idea but at some point in the early 1880s he began to feel that a Parliament in Dublin might be the solution. In December 1885 he allowed his conversion to Home Rule to become known. This had a profound impact on domestic British politics. The Conservatives, led by Lord Salisbury, adopted a staunchly oppositional role, inspired by the maverick Tory Lord Randolph Churchill's rallying cry that 'Ulster will fight and Ulster will be right'. The Liberal Party was badly split on the issue and eventually ninety-three dissident Liberals voted against the bill. The net effect was disastrous for both the Liberals and Ireland: the Liberal Party remained split, with two of Gladstone's possible successors, Lord Hartington and Joseph Chamberlain, in the break-away Liberal Unionists. Parnell had failed to deliver Home Rule and before he could try again his political career was wrecked when a member of his party, Captain O'Shea, filed for divorce, citing Parnell as the man with whom his wife had been unfaithful. In fact the O'Shea marriage had long since been finished in all but legal name and for several years Parnell and Katharine O'Shea had lived together, referring to each other as husband and wife. But Catholic Ireland was more concerned with public morality than with private realities and Parnell's career did not recover from the scandal. In 1891 Parnell died, his health having been ruined in a winter campaign in Ireland to try to win back the support of the people.

Home Rule lived on as an idea and Gladstone's second attempt in 1893 actually passed its various stages in the Commons before being rejected by the Lords. It would return in 1912.

ANALYSIS (1): WHY DID PROBLEMS OVER LAND IN IRELAND PROVOKE SUCH DIFFICULTIES FOR THE BRITISH GOVERNMENT BETWEEN 1877 AND 1886?

The Land War of 1879–82 can be thought of as a struggle between the landlords and the tenantry, the latter being organised into the Irish National Land League. The focal point of the League was the charismatic president Charles Stewart Parnell, but the real founder of the League, and to some extent its chief tactician, was Michael Davitt, an exceptionally able nationalist with a Fenian background.

Davitt later went on to write a history of the Land Question in Ireland and it is from such sources that some of the most potent mythologies have subsequently grown. Davitt depicted the Land War in black and white: as a struggle between a ruthlessly exploitative landlord class, whom he described as 'cormorant vampires',[1] and a downtrodden mass of poor farmers given heroic leadership by the Land League. This picture has been progressively redrawn by modern historians and, thanks largely to the revisionists and their opponents, the historiographical image is now rather more grey. In order to achieve some sort of clarity it is perhaps necessary to go back to economic basics.

It is important to remember that the long-term effect of the famine was not only to alleviate pressure on the land but also to allow land consolidation among tenant farmers, to the extent that the 1850s and 1860s can be seen as something of a boom time for many of Ireland's middle-ranking tenant farmers. Many historians have therefore described the subsequent Land War as something brought about not by abject poverty but by the relatively sudden ending of a period of prosperity.

The primary cause of this reversal was the so-called Great Agricultural Depression of the mid-1870s onwards. The depression was caused by a number of factors beginning with harvest failure in

1877, partial failure in 1878 and freak weather conditions. In addition to this the invasion of British markets by American grain and beef, as the great farming belt of the American mid-west was opened up, created a situation in which agricultural prices were falling and as a result tenant farmers were increasingly unable to meet rental demands. In this way the depression created a situation in which both tenant farmer and landlord suffered. Only the genuinely poor benefited from cheaper food prices.

The response of landlords to the depression was inevitable. The traditional sins of this alleged 'vampire' class – rack-renting, absenteeism and evictions – were not perhaps the heartless acts of a profiteering ruling class but the desperate response of an increasingly indebted group in the face of new economic realities which showed every sign of creating a long-term structural crisis.

What made this Irish problem eventually a problem for the British government was the fact that committed nationalists, of all sorts, saw in this crisis the possibilities of a new mass campaign: the first large-scale mobilisation of the people since the days of O'Connell. The first to see the possibilities in this crisis was Michael Davitt. Tenant leagues had long existed at a local level in Ireland but in 1879 Davitt forged the creation of the first national tenant league: the Irish National Land League. But Davitt's masterstroke was to persuade Charles Stewart Parnell, the up-and-coming Irish nationalist MP for County Meath, to take the presidency of the new organisation.

Parnell was undoubtedly the pivotal figure in Anglo-Irish relations over the next decade. He had an astonishing ability to pull together the various strands of Irish nationalism into a focused movement able to exert extraordinary pressure on the British government. By 1879 Parnell was both president of the new Land League and a leading figure in the Irish Parliamentary Party (IPP) at Westminster. At this juncture the Irish Parliamentary Party was led by the moderate Isaac Butt with the vaguely stated aim of trying to achieve some sort of Home Rule for Ireland. Traditionally Irish nationalists had been divided between moderates like Butt or O'Connell, who rejected violence, and men of violence such as the Young Irelanders and the Fenians. Parnell's achievement was to build a bridge between these traditions. Even before being appointed president of the Land League, Parnell had been exploring links with the Fenian movement in America. Eventually, with the support of the leading American Fenian, John Devoy, Parnell obtained a Fenian pledge of support for his leadership. For a brief moment the Irish nationalist cause, diverse and contradictory as it was, had one clear leader. Devoy christened this moment the 'New Departure'.[2]

In order to appease the more militant segments of the nationalist movement Parnell needed to devise aggressive strategies without actually sanctioning violence. Broadly, Parnell pursued multiple, simultaneous tactics, each of which in differing ways was designed to force the British government to wake up to Irish grievances and demands, particularly over land issues, but also ultimately over the issue of Home Rule. As the land campaign began to unfold in Ireland, Parnell sought ways of directing Westminster's attention to Ireland. To this end, he joined in with and then came to lead the campaign which came to be known as 'obstruction'. This involved the making of interminable speeches by a handful of Irish MPs with the deliberate aim of paralysing the Parliamentary process – a technique Americans were later to call filibustering. Pioneered by an Ulsterman called Joseph Biggar, with an unintelligible accent, it was perfected under Parnell. In this irritating manner the Irish talked their way on to England's agenda.

In Ireland itself, Parnell devised a plan for the Land League. In 1880 in a speech at Ennis he advocated sending those landlords who seemed to be harsh on their tenants to what he called a 'moral Coventry'. In practice this meant a refusal to cooperate or even communicate with such landlords or their agents. The first significant victim of this strategy was the agent of Lord Mayo, one Captain Boycott, a man who unwittingly gave his name to this method.

Gladstone was returned as Prime Minister in 1880. Parnell's tactics and the general unrest in Ireland persuaded Gladstone to consider further land legislation. The first Land Act of 1870 had largely failed to solve the problems and the depression highlighted the need to do more. His solution was the 1881 Land Act which delivered the so-called 3Fs, the long-standing demand of Ireland's tenant leagues. In many ways this was a brave move by Gladstone which risked accusations of weakness in the face of extra-Parliamentary pressure. Indeed, his Irish Secretary, W.E. Forster, was so unhappy with the concessionary approach that he resigned.

But difficulties remained. Parnell had been interned in Kilmainham prison in 1881 for inciting disorder, under the government's Coercion Act. Parnell was delighted at his incarceration as it increased his credibility with the Fenians but, surprisingly, he was also able to continue orchestrating the land campaign from his cell; from it he was also able to open lines of negotiation with Gladstone, through various intermediaries. At this point he simultaneously urged the members of the Land League not to pay any rent, in order to drive the crisis to some sort of conclusion.

This no-rent policy created problems beyond anything offered by Gladstone's second Land Act. Landlords inevitably demanded the rental arrears. Thus the land problem could not be fully settled unless this issue could be solved. To add to the complexities of the situation, there was a sense in which Parnell and Davitt did not want a solution, finding the Land League a most useful engine with which to drive forward the nationalist movement as a whole. It was perhaps this last point which pushed Gladstone to yet greater levels of governmental generosity. After a period of shadowy nego- tiation by proxy with the imprisoned Parnell, Parliament eventually passed the Arrears Act of May 1882 by which the government itself paid off the arrears. The Act has become known, rather mis- leadingly, as the Kilmainham Treaty. It was not a treaty as such and more Gladstone's idea than Parnell's but it was another brave piece of Irish appeasement by the Liberal leader, and it was to bring fresh difficulties in its wake.

Four days after Parnell was released from prison and the news of the Kilmainham Treaty hit the newspapers, the new Irish Chief Secretary, Lord Frederick Cavendish, and his Under-Secretary, Burke, were brutally hacked to death in Dublin's Phoenix Park by a Fenian splinter group calling itself the Invincibles. Suddenly it seemed that Gladstone had been making deals with murderers, or at least that his weakness had only served to encourage the wilder nationalists. There was outrage in the press. But Gladstone remained firm, even turning down Parnell's offer of resignation from the leadership of the Irish party. Between them they endured the storm, and in retrospect the Phoenix Park murders appear as an isolated atrocity amid a period of progress.

Gladstone's Land and Arrears Acts were fairly successful in bringing the Land War to a close and indeed in derailing the Land League. But ironically it was to be the Conservative Party which drove the Land Question towards a more satisfying conclusion.

By 1885 it had become clear that the demand for Home Rule was the new focus of the nationalist movement. The Conservatives under Lord Salisbury were not enthusiastic about this, though they kept their views to themselves until Gladstone finally committed himself. But during the brief Salisbury ministry of the second half of 1885, the Conservative Irish Secretary, Lord Ashbourne, developed an approach to Irish policy which became known as Constructive Unionism. In short, the Conservatives hoped to win Irish support

for the Union and, by implication, undermine the Home Rule movement by offering major concessions on the land issue. The 1885
Ashbourne Act provided government loans to Irish tenant farmers
to help them buy their farms from their landlords. This approach
culminated in the 1903 Wyndham Act which not only provided
loans but guaranteed that the repayments would be lower than
rentals, thereby causing an almost revolutionary change in patterns
of land ownership. But if the Conservatives hoped this would buy off
the nationalist call for Home Rule, they were to be proved wrong.
Evidently, though the land issue had helped to awaken a nationalist
desire for Home Rule, the land issue could not be so simply used to
extinguish the idea.

Questions

1. Assess Michael Davitt's contribution to the Irish nationalist cause.
2. How successful was Gladstone in resolving difficulties in
   Ireland between 1868 and 1882?
3. What, if anything, did the Fenians achieve?

ANALYSIS (2): WHO GAINED AND WHO LOST IN THE BATTLE FOR HOME RULE BETWEEN 1885 AND 1894?

Given the complex manoeuvring and counter-manoeuvring that
characterised the politics of the Home Rule crisis, it is tempting to
see it as something of a game, albeit for high stakes. Indeed, Lord
Randolph Churchill's quip about playing the 'Orange card' would
seem to add validity to this idea.[3] If it was a game, as Churchill's
metaphor implies, an obvious question asserts itself: who won?

Parnell was playing for the biggest prize: self-government for
Ireland and his claim that he had a Parliament for Ireland 'within
the hollow of my hand' suggests that he felt that he was extremely
close to his aim.[4] But the awkward fact remains that an Irish Parliament did not materialise during his lifetime. So does this mean that
Parnell simply failed?

Undoubtedly Parnell had a string of considerable achievements to
his name before 1885. He had transformed the Irish Parliamentary
Party into a disciplined machine, demanding of his fellow Irish
MPs that they sign the infamous pledge which committed them to

supporting the party line, a line inevitably dictated by Parnell. He had extracted from Gladstone a Land Act in 1881 which delivered the long-sought-after demands of tenant organisations in Ireland and even managed to get the British government to pick up the rent arrears caused by his 'No Rent' policy. In addition to that, he had succeeded in persuading most within the Fenian movement to accept non-violent political methods, which gave a certain air of respectability to the cause and thereby allowed even Conservative administrations to consider doing business with Irish nationalists: an achievement capable even of withstanding the political storm caused by the Phoenix Park murders. But all that said, he failed to deliver Home Rule. Why?

The short answer is simply that in 1886 the Liberal Party split over the issue of Home Rule and the ninety-three Liberal Unionists, combined with Conservatives and Ulster Unionists, proved enough to sink the bill. But even if the bill had survived the Commons it is certain that the House of Lords would have vetoed the idea. After all, this is exactly what happened when Gladstone put forward a second Home Rule bill in 1893. In that sense, given the natural Conservative and Unionist majority in the upper house, it is sometimes tempting to see Gladstone's efforts as a kind of exercise in futility: maybe even a pretence designed to buy Parnell's support in the lower house. But this would be unfair to both men. Both the Liberal leader and the Irish Chief Secretary knew they were playing a long game. Ultimately perhaps this was Parnell's greatest achievement: by 1886 he had helped to convince not just Gladstone but also a majority of the Liberals that Ireland deserved self-government. Unfortunately this had the immediate effect of splitting the Liberals and ushering in the age of Salisbury and Balfour. Even here Parnell's ghost might have savoured the fruits of the Conservative Party's policy of 'Constructive Unionism', the highlight of which was the generous land purchase schemes offered in the Wyndham Act of 1903. But it is surely the fact that both Gladstone and later Asquith tried again to achieve Home Rule that suggests that Parnell had achieved something politically durable. Home Rule, in some form, would certainly have become a reality in 1914 if the Great War had not intervened. In that sense, the war robbed Parnell of a greater place in the history of Anglo-Irish relations.

Before looking at the other party leaders, Gladstone and Salisbury, it is perhaps appropriate to consider the respective roles of the two younger men within the parties: Joseph Chamberlain for the Liberals and Lord Randolph Churchill for the Conservatives, both of whom were young ambitious politicians determined to twist the possibilities of Home Rule to their advantage.

Lord Randolph Churchill was an aristocratic Tory but one so unruly and undisciplined that he and his clique were known as the 'Fourth Party'. On Irish issues he was seen as something of an expert, having worked as private secretary to his father in Ireland during the latter's Lord Lieutenancy between 1876 and 1879. More than that, his first-hand experience of Irish problems was rumoured to have made him deeply sympathetic towards Irish nationalism in general. This, taken with his reputation as something of a rebel, certainly led Parnell to see in Churchill a man who might swing the Conservatives behind Home Rule. Allegedly, there were a number of clandestine meetings between the two men in late 1885, no record of which now exists. And yet as soon as Gladstone declared in favour of Home Rule, it was Churchill who rallied the Conservatives to the Orange flag. Indeed, with his famous inflammatory speech to the Orange Order in February 1886 ('Ulster will fight and Ulster will be right') Churchill established the Tory line on Ireland for the next century. Inevitably, it has been argued that this was simply cynical party gamesmanship. Certainly A.B. Cooke and J.R. Vincent, in their classic account of the Home Rule crisis *The Governing Passion*, see Churchill as being 'greatly more concerned with party alignments than with Irish unrest'.[5] In this scenario Churchill was simply using the Home Rule issue as an arena in which he might demonstrate his ability to lead Conservative opinion and thereby stake his claim to the future leadership of the party. This may be unfair. It is also possible to see Churchill as a man with a family history of what is usually called 'enlightened or constructive Unionism'; in other words, the historiographical arguments have centred upon whether his actions in 1886 should be seen as consistent or cynically calculating. There is not the space to debate the issue here but what is clear is that Churchill gave a crucial lead to Salisbury and his party. After the fall of Gladstone, Churchill was rewarded by Salisbury with a prize Cabinet position as Chancellor of the Exchequer. But such was Churchill's restless nature that within a matter of months he had argued with Salisbury and resigned. Salisbury was too shrewd to bring him back and the onset of syphilitic madness destroyed what was left of his career.

There is a certain symmetry about Joseph Chamberlain's relationship with Gladstone and Churchill's with Salisbury. Chamberlain was also a younger man in a hurry who may have seized upon the Home Rule crisis as a great political opportunity. Chamberlain had forged his reputation in the preceding years as the emerging leader of radical liberalism. After the 1884 Reform Act two-thirds of men had the vote; the age of mass politics had begun. Many in the Liberal Party felt that Chamberlain's particular brand of welfare policies – he championed better housing for the poor, better education and a fairer taxation system – represented the kind of popular policies that would help Liberals triumph in a democratic age. But Chamberlain's radical programme was not adopted by Gladstone. To Chamberlain and his followers Home Rule was an irritating side-show. Whether Chamberlain sought to bring down Gladstone over Home Rule in order to clear the way for his own policies, and for his own ascent to the leadership, is highly debatable. What is clear is that after Gladstone declared in favour of some sort of Home Rule measure in late 1885, Chamberlain rapidly became one of the leading oppositional voices in the Liberal Party. He objected on numerous grounds. Home Rule might weaken the empire. The complete removal of Irish MPs from Westminster, as Gladstone proposed, would undermine the British Parliament and create difficulties over taxation – how could Westminster raise taxes in Ireland if Ireland had no MPs? This would be taxation without representation, the very grievance that had stoked the revolt of the American colonies in 1776. He was also quick to jump on Churchill's bandwagon about the rights of Protestants in Ulster. Just how genuine his objections were is very hard to say. He was undoubtedly ambitious but he was also frustrated that Gladstone had chosen to reduce Liberalism to this one unpopular issue, ignoring the grievances of the English working classes, many of whom now had the vote. Arguably Gladstone was preventing the development of Liberalism. Whatever Chamberlain's motives, it is clear that he was one of the leaders of the Liberal opposition on the third reading of Gladstone's bill (ninety-three Liberals voted against) and that he was therefore in part responsible for its failure. Chamberlain gained little from the manoeuvre. Oddly enough, the bulk of the radical Liberals stayed with Gladstone. It was the right wing of the party, the so-called Whig faction, that dominated the rebel group, under the leadership of Lord Hartington. Instead of toppling Gladstone, Chamberlain had somehow separated himself from his followers. There were attempts to bring him back into the Liberal fold but his disloyalty to Gladstone had offended too many. He was left at the helm of a group soon to be known as the Liberal Unionists: an ideologically incoherent grouping with little future. If Chamberlain had played a game in 1886 he had certainly lost. Ironically enough, he eventually drifted into the Tories, only to split them over tariff reform in 1902–3.

It might also be thought that Gladstone had hardly come out of the crisis with much to his credit. He failed to deliver Home Rule for Ireland. He failed again in 1893. To make matters worse he split his party, something which ushered in twenty years of Tory domination. The split deprived the party of its most obvious future leader: Joseph Chamberlain. It can also be argued that it was partly because of this weakness and the party's failure to develop the kind of radicalism preached by Chamberlain that the need for a new sort of party established itself amongst the lower classes. Therefore it might be said that Gladstone held the Liberals back and thereby, indirectly, allowed a left-wing party to emerge, the Labour Party, that would eventually usurp the Liberal position. All of this would mean that Gladstone not only lost over Home Rule but condemned his party to even greater defeats in the future. But this is probably projecting too far ahead.

Gladstone had achieved much by 1886. He had established the idea of Home Rule and perhaps even put it permanently on the Liberal agenda. Even after the defeat of the second bill in 1893 Gladstone could point to the fact that the bill had passed through the Commons and only failed in the Lords. In that sense Gladstone had moved the idea forward. It can also be argued that he was quite happy to see the Lords obstruct the Commons because it gave fuel to his argument that the powers of the Lords needed to be reduced. It must also be pointed out that Gladstone was a shrewd politician and that he wanted to use the crisis to out-manoeuvre his rivals. It would be unfair to suggest that he planned it, but certainly Gladstone subsequently declared his satisfaction with the political exile of Chamberlain. In that sense Gladstone was an old man in a hurry. Indeed it could be argued that Gladstone's real mission was to pacify the Liberal Party. In a way, then, Gladstone was a winner. He had advanced the cause of Home Rule and seen off his nearest political rival. But the negative consequences of Home Rule, for the Liberal Party, at least suggest that it was something of a flawed victory.

The leader of the Conservative Party, Lord Salisbury, was the least active of all the protagonists. Before Gladstone made his views known, Salisbury was careful to keep his utterances as ambiguous as possible. So nervous was he of giving a clear opinion that the historian F.S.L. Lyons has aptly described him as being like 'an elephant walking on eggshells'.[6] It was Churchill who jolted the party into its Unionist stance in February 1886 but after that Salisbury rapidly warmed to his new-found role as defender of Protestant liberties. Once liberated, Salisbury made it clear that not only was he hostile to Home Rule, he had a very low opinion of the Catholic or Celtic Irish in general, describing them as being like 'Hottentots'. But in many ways it was Salisbury's characteristic unflappability which helped him the most. Whilst Gladstone and Chamberlain squabbled and wrecked the Liberals, and Churchill and Parnell wrecked themselves, Salisbury began to find himself in the strongest political position. Thus we are left with the irony that the politician who seemed to care the least about Ireland, and cared least about his popularity with the masses, emerged from the struggles as the most successful political player.

Questions

1. Does Parnell deserve his reputation as one of the great Irish nationalist leaders?
2. Why did Home Rule prove to be such a divisive issue in British politics?

SOURCES

1. THE PROBLEMS POSED BY THE FENIANS AND THE LAND LEAGUE

Source A: R. Kee, *The Bold Fenian Men* (London: Weidenfeld & Nicolson, 1972), an account of the consequences of the Fenian attack on a police van in Manchester in 1867.

Large numbers of Irishmen in Manchester were soon rounded up. The identification procedure employed by the police was so questionable that the surprising thing was not that one of the five men eventually put on trial for their lives should be entirely innocent but that the other four were in fact all involved in one way or another in the rescue attempt. In court it was repeatedly maintained that Allen had fired the final shot. In fact this was not so and the man, Rice, who did, had escaped. But in English law it was immaterial who had fired the shot, for anyone taking part in an illegal act as a result of which someone is killed was guilty of constructive murder. Allen, Larkin and O'Brien were executed in public on the foggy morning of

24 November 1867, Larkin and O'Brien suffering much agony as a result of bungling on the part of the hangman.

Source B: M. Davitt, *The Fall of Feudalism* (London and New York: Harper & Bros, 1904).

Almost my first remembered experience of my own life and of the existence of Landlordism was our eviction in 1852, when I was about five years of age. That eviction and the privations of the preceding Famine years, the story of the starving peasantry of Mayo, of the deaths from hunger and the coffinless graves on the roadside – everywhere a hole could be dug for the slaves who died because of 'God's providence' – all this was the political food seasoned with a mother's tears over unmerited sorrows and sufferings which had fed my mind in another land.

Source C: Charles Parnell's speech at Ennis, quoted in *The Freeman's Journal*, 20 September 1880.

Now, what are you to do to a tenant who bids for a farm from which another tenant has been evicted? (Several voices shout: 'shoot him') I think I heard someone say shoot him. (Cheers) I wish to point out to you a very much better way – a more Christian and charitable way, which will give the lost man an opportunity of repenting (laughter). When a man takes a farm from which another has been evicted you must shun him on the roadside when you meet him – you must shun him in the streets of the town – you must shun him in the shop – you must shun him in the fairgreen and in the market place, and even in the place of worship, by leaving him alone, by putting him in a Moral Coventry, by isolating him from the rest of his country as if he were the leper of old – you must show him your detestation of the crime he has committed.

Source D: J. Bardon, *A History of Ulster* (Belfast: Blackstaff Press, 1992).

Captain Charles Boycott, agent for Lord Erne's Mayo Estate, became a celebrated victim [of Parnell's 'Moral Coventry' policy] when he described his plight in a letter to *The Times*. Ulster Conservatives, fervently supported by the *Belfast Newsletter*, determined to lead an armed expedition of Orangemen to Connacht to lift Boycott's potato crop and thrash his corn. The alarmed chief secretary William E. Forster rushed seven thousand troops to Mayo, including Surgeon-Major Reynolds VC, hero of Rorke's Drift the year before. Twenty five Protestant labourers from Co. Monaghan joined twenty five Protestant labourers from Co. Cavan at Clones Station on Thursday 11 November 1880, where for fear of 'the bludgeon men of Mayo' they were each given a revolver.

Source E: A letter from Charles Parnell to Katharine O'Shea on the morning of his arrest, 13 October 1881.

My own Queenie, I have just been arrested by two fine looking detectives, and write these words to wifie to tell her that she must be a brave little woman and not fret after her husband. The only thing that makes me worried and unhappy is that it may hurt you or our child.

You know, darling, that on this account it will be wicked of you to grieve, as I can never have any other wife but you, and if anything happens to you I must die childless. Be good and brave, dear little wifie then.

Your own husband.[7]

Politically it is a fortunate thing for me that I have been arrested, as the movement is breaking fast, and all will be quiet in a few months, when I shall be released.

Questions

1. Explain the following phrases:
   (i) 'all this was the political food' (Source B). (2 marks)
   (ii) 'politically it is a fortunate thing for me' (Source E). (2 marks)
2. How useful is Source C as evidence that Parnell rejected the idea of using physical force? (5 marks)
*3. Use Source A and your own knowledge to discuss the view that the arrest, trial and execution of the 'Manchester Martyrs' was a miscarriage of justice? (7 marks)
4. Use Sources C, D and E to assess the view that the Irish National Land League was not as strong in Ireland as is often supposed. (9 marks)

Worked answer

*3. Source A goes some way towards substantiating the nationalist view that the executed men at Manchester were in some ways victims of an injustice themselves and therefore martyrs to their cause. There is a clear suggestion that police methods used in identifying and rounding up possible Irish suspects were, as Kee politely puts it, 'questionable'. One of the five men eventually charged, Maguire, an Irish marine on leave and entirely ignorant of Fenian matters, seems to have been arrested purely for being Irish.

Nevertheless, despite the miscarriage of justice obviously involved in his case – he was after all found guilty – he was eventually pardoned. More significantly perhaps, no evidence was produced to prove that any of the men found guilty actually fired a weapon, let alone intended to kill the police sergeant. It is plainly stated in the source that real killer, Rice, had escaped. The additional detail at the end of the piece about the 'bungling' of the hangman apparently confirms that at every stage of the legal operation, from identification through to execution, the men had not received what might reasonably be called justice.

However, Kee does admit that the police were actually remarkably successful in that four out of the five men charged were involved, 'in one way or another'. It can also be argued that the sentence was not a miscarriage given that the criminal law, at the time, contained the crime of 'constructive murder' of which four of the men would seem to have been guilty. In that sense, by the standards of the time there was no miscarriage. Even the bungling of the hangman was at worst an unfortunate accident. It can be objected that the law at the time was simply designed to make it easier for the state to remove its enemies. Seen in that light, of course, one man's justice is another man's colonial oppression and conclusions are simply opinions.

Perhaps the oddest element in the affair, and perhaps even the most unfair, is the fact that the fourth man, Edward Condon, though clearly as guilty as the three hanged men – indeed he later bragged of how he had 'masterminded' the rescue – was reprieved at the last moment because he was an American citizen – not unlike de Valera in 1916. In this respect at least, there was some small grain of truth in the old nationalist cliché that the real crime of the Fenian rebels was to be Irish.

2. THE STRUGGLE OVER HOME RULE IN 1886

Source F: A Letter from Lord Randolph Churchill to Lord Justice Fitzgibbon, 16 February 1886.

I decided some time ago that if the GOM [the Grand Old Man, i.e. Gladstone] went for Home Rule, the Orange Card would be the one to play. Please God may it turn out the ace of trumps and not the two.

Source G: Speech by Gladstone in Parliament, 7 June 1886.

I cannot conceal the conviction that the voice of Ireland, as a whole, is at this moment clearly and constitutionally spoken. I cannot say it otherwise when five-sixths of its lawfully chosen representatives are of one mind on the matter. Certainly, sir, I cannot allow it to be said that a Protestant minority in Ulster, or elsewhere, is to rule the question at large for Ireland.

Source H: Extracts from A.B. Cooke and J.R. Vincent's *The Governing Passion* (Brighton: Harvester Press, 1974).

Gladstone was presented with an opportunity of securing his ministers' assent to the principle of the exclusion of Chamberlain (alias Home Rule). . . . The Home Rule bill, as hastily put together as a Disraeli Reform bill, was hardly meant to establish Home Rule. All the classic objections – the Lords, the lateness of the session, the drafting problems – were obvious . . . All that in the end can be said about Gladstone's short term political motives, is that he wished to recapture control of his party.

Source I: Salisbury on Gladstone's idea that it was important to have confidence in the Irish people. From a speech to the National Union of Conservative and Constitutional Associations, 15 May 1886.

Confidence depends upon the people in whom you are to confide. You would not confide free representative institutions to the Hottentots [an African tribal group], for instance. Nor, going higher up the scale, would you confide them to the oriental nations whom you are governing in India . . . This which is called self-government, but which is really government by the majority, works admirably well when it is confided to the people who are of Teutonic race, but it does not work so well when people of other races are called upon to join in it.

Source J: From Parnell's speech in Cork, 21 January 1885.

I do not know whether England will be wise in time and concede to constitutional arguments and methods the restitution of that which was stolen from us towards the close of the last century. It is given to none of us to forecast the future . . . no man has the right to fix the boundary to the march of a nation. No man has a right to say to his country, 'Thus far shalt thou go and no further', and we have never attempted to fix the *ne plus ultra* to the progress of Ireland's nationhood.

Source K: Parnell speaking in Parliament during the closing stages of the debate on Gladstone's bill, 7 June 1886.

We [the Irish Party] look upon the provisions of the bill as a final settlement of this question, and . . . I believe that the Irish people have accepted it as such a settlement. (cheers and ironical cheers) Of course you may not believe me, but I can say no more.

Questions

1. Explain the meaning of the following phrases in their given context:
   (i) 'Hottentots' (Source I). (2 marks)
   (ii) 'you may not believe me' (Source K). (2 marks)
2. Explain why Source H is often seen as a controversial view. (5 marks)
*3. Compare Sources F and G. What do they reveal about the differing ways in which Churchill and Gladstone approached the Ulster question? (7 marks)
4. Use these sources to assess the view that Home Rule meant very different things to different people. (9 marks)

Worked answer

*3. In many respects the two sources confirm the traditional pictures of Gladstone as the morally earnest, political pilgrim and Churchill as the cynical and faintly corrupt political adventurer.

Certainly the language of the Churchill source is revealing. The famous quip about 'playing the Orange Card' can surely only be the statement of a man who was playing political games for his own ends, indifferent to the moral rights and wrongs of the situation. The apparent fact that his commitment to the Orange cause was brought about only because it happened to be the most convenient means of opposing Gladstone again suggests that his concern for the Protestants was rather disingenuous.

Gladstone, by contrast, would appear to have been driven by higher moral purposes. His lofty phrase about the 'voice of Ireland' is clearly a reference to the election of 1885 in which 'five-sixths' of the MPs returned from Ireland were from Parnell's party. Evidently Gladstone felt that to reject this lawful expression of Irish nationalism would be to run the risk of encouraging a return to the old physical-force traditions of the Fenians. Although it is possible to argue that Gladstone was also playing his own political game, as Cooke and Vincent do in Source H, there seems little reason to doubt that this source reveals his basic attitude to the Ulster problem. Fundamentally, as the source implies, Gladstone saw Ireland as one nation and thus the Protestants in the north could never be more than a 'minority'. Churchill saw Ireland as two nations. Although Gladstone's view seems logical and indeed principled, styles can be deceiving. Churchill's language suggests indifference and opportunism but, irrespective of that, the fact remains that he had seen into the heart of the problem in a way that Gladstone, for all his rhetoric, had not. In fact what these sources expose most clearly is the varieties of political obtuseness about Ulster existing in Westminster. Gladstone saw the seriousness of the problem but failed to understand it, while Churchill grasped the problem but saw it as relatively trivial. Ironically history would turn these various party positions on their head. In the generation after Gladstone, the Liberals steadily lost their certainty that Ireland was one nation, reaching the point where Asquith was ready to give some part of Ulster some sort of opt-out of Home Rule in 1914, whilst the opportunistic Tories gradually acquired convictions, culminating in Bonar Law's extremely passionate commitment to the Loyalist cause in the period 1912 to 1914. In that sense these two sources, whilst revealing a lot about the dispositions of the two men, also distort as much as they reveal about the whole issue in the longer term.

5

CULTURAL NATIONALISM AND UNIONISM, 1890–1914

BACKGROUND NARRATIVE

The Parnell scandal had the effect of splitting the Irish Parliamentary Party (IPP) into pro- and anti-Parnell factions. The bitterness of this division meant that for almost twenty years the IPP was relatively weak. Nationalists grew frustrated at the party's internal bickering and the nationalist movement began slowly to turn away from conventional politics. At the risk of oversimplification, Irish nationalism after Parnell shifted away from the political towards more cultural forms of action.

In practice this involved the emergence of a journalism and a literature which sought to disparage all things English and Protestant and to propagate and praise all things deemed to be Gaelic and/or Catholic and therefore, in the eyes of the new cultural nationalists, genuinely Irish. The leaders of this Gaelic or Celtic revival felt that the 'real' Ireland was the ancient Ireland that had existed before the waves of foreign invasion imposed an 'alien' religion and culture. The task for such cultural nationalists would be to rediscover the ancient Gaelic civilisation of Ireland's past, the better to prepare for Ireland's return to her true self in the future.

At first some of the new organisations may seem a little distant from nationalist politics. For example, the first major movement to push for the revival of Gaelic ideals was the Gaelic Athletic

Association (GAA), a body designed to stimulate interest in Gaelic sports, such as hockey, hurling and Gaelic football. Other sports such as cricket and association football were demonised as English games. Though it may seem unlikely that independence can be won with a hurling stick, it interesting to note that the militant and secretive nationalist organisation known as the Irish Republican Brotherhood (IRB) or 'Fenians' gradually infiltrated the GAA, using it as both a useful propaganda machine and a recruiting ground.

But the most significant catalyst of this new nationalism was undoubtedly the Gaelic League, formed in 1893. The League grew very slowly at first but by the first decade of the twentieth century its membership had risen to one hundred thousand. Nevertheless this still meant that the League was a relatively small movement and, given that its leader, Douglas Hyde, specifically rejected the idea of seeking to use it for political ends – preferring to assert that the most important work was the reviving of the Gaelic language and the collecting of Celtic folk tales – it is quite difficult to assess how much the League promoted the nationalist cause.

It is an odd fact that at precisely the time that this Gaelic revival began, there was also an extraordinary flowering of brilliant literary works by Irishmen writing in English. In some ways the works of people like W.B. Yeats and J.M. Synge drew heavily upon the new interest in ancient Ireland and also helped to further stimulate national pride. But it is also true that these writers were artists before they were nationalists and much of their work was not welcomed by the more zealous patriots. Famously, Synge's *Playboy of the Western World* caused a riot in the new Irish National Theatre in Dublin in 1907 because it portrayed the western peasantry in a poor light.

The result of the elections of 1910, however, breathed new life into the more traditional political nationalism of the IPP. By chance, they found themselves holding the balance of power between the Liberals and the Conservatives. The Liberals now depended upon the IPP in order to stay in government. In what the Conservative leader, Bonar Law, called a 'corrupt bargain', Asquith committed his party to put forward a Home Rule bill and the IPP agreed to support the Liberals in their social policies. The fact that the Parliament Act of 1911 also removed the Lords' power of veto over proposed legislation meant that the upper house, which had a large

Unionist majority, was no longer able to guarantee the failure of Home Rule. Thus by 1911 it was clear that a Parliament in Dublin, with limited but significant rights to govern Ireland, was a realistic possibility. This in turn revitalised the Unionist opposition to Home Rule both in Ulster and in Conservative circles in the British establishment.

The leader of the Unionist movement was Edward Carson, a Protestant lawyer from Dublin. Carson's preferred solution was for all Ireland to remain one entity within the Union and for Home Rule to be blocked in its entirety. As events unfolded, however, and it became clear that Unionism was weak as a political force almost everywhere except Ulster, Carson concluded that if the Union could not be saved as a whole it could be defended most effectively in Ulster.

In 1912 Carson manufactured one of the great demonstrations of Ulster Protestant hostility to Home Rule by drafting the so-called 'Solemn League and Covenant' which pledged all the signatories to 'use all means which may be found necessary' to defeat any attempt to introduce Home Rule. On 28 September 1912 in Belfast and elsewhere in Ulster, the Protestant Ulstermen and women turned out to sign the pledge, some of them doing so in their own blood. Evidently the Liberal government, having introduced the Home Rule bill for its first reading earlier in the year, was now on a collision course with Ulster.

To make this situation all the more explosive, the Conservative Party under Bonar Law was not only supporting the Unionists but using the same sort of threatening and inflammatory rhetoric; all of which seemed to suggest that a civil war might be looming. Certainly nationalists and Unionists seemed to be preparing for just that. In 1913 the Ulster Unionists formed the Ulster Volunteer Force, a private militia, with the aim of resisting Home Rule with force if necessary. This development was mirrored in the nationalist camp with the creation of the Irish Volunteers and James Connolly's own Irish Marxist militia, the Irish Citizen Army. Behind these two armed nationalist bodies lurked the presence of the IRB. Imperial Germany, with an agenda of its own, generously provided weapons for both sides.

The politicians flapped around looking for compromises. The idea that Ulster was different and might be treated slightly differently was established in that very period. But no one could find a formula to appease all sides. In the event the solution to the crisis arrived in the form of the Great War. When war broke out Asquith took the opportunity to suspend the Home Rule legislation for the duration of the hostilities. Men from both sides rushed to join up. For a moment there was no Irish question.

ANALYSIS (1): CULTURAL NATIONALISM WAS MORE INFLUENTIAL THAN TRADITIONAL POLITICAL NATIONALISM BETWEEN 1891 AND 1914. DISCUSS.

Cultural change is, by its nature, hard to quantify. It may even be said that there was not a singular cultural revival at this time but instead a myriad of excitements, each of which can only just be squeezed under the banner of revivalism. Nevertheless, so long as it is remembered that the Gaelic revival of 1890 to 1914 was a diverse phenomenon and one that was not political in the conventional sense, then it may be possible to discuss its political impact.

From a certain angle, the Gaelic movement can appear profoundly influential: the seed-bed of a revolution that would burst upon Ireland in the Easter of 1916 and culminate in the Anglo-Irish Treaty of 1921. It is certainly true that many of the key players in those subsequent dramas, such as Patrick Pearse, Michael Collins and Eamon de Valera, all claimed to have been inspired by the ideas promulgated by the Gaelic League. Collins stated that the language question was to be his first priority after the Anglo-Irish Treaty of 1921 was signed. We also know that about 50 per cent of the Free State's first generation of political leaders had been members of the Gaelic League. Indeed Douglas Hyde was made President of Ireland in 1938. Clearly then, there is a case for arguing that the League was a nursery for nationalist revolutionaries.

Once the Gaelic revival is perceived in this light it becomes easy to see many of the cultural manifestations associated with the movement as part of a covert revolutionary strategy. The Gaelic Athletic Association, with its call to hurling and Gaelic football, becomes a marvellous means of politicising the masses without requiring of them too much thought or commitment.

But perhaps the most weighty claim that can be made for the cultural renaissance is that the emphasis on pre-Reformation culture alienated Protestants and eventually made the partition of Ireland inevitable. In that sense the triumph of the Gaelicist ideals effectively killed the old Toneite belief in a united Ireland. Though there were numerous Protestants among the early membership of the Gaelic League – including, surprisingly enough, Hyde himself – the bigoted language of such aggressively Catholic journalists as D.P. Moran (he called Irish Protestants 'sourfaced foreigners') in the 1890s and the whole logic of the Gaelicist standpoint virtually guaranteed a corresponding Protestant bigotry. There is some irony in this, given that Hyde, the son of Protestant rector, occasionally professed to believe that the joy of discovering their ancient culture might be a means of uniting all Irishmen of all creeds.

But Hyde was a little naive. In the mouths of less refined gentlemen than him, his ideas took on a sectarian and racialist character that bred the hatred and extremism that took violent shape in 1916.

However, the importance of the Gaelic revival can be overstressed. It should be remembered that it was always a minority movement, perhaps even a faintly risible one: a respectable hobby for numbers of petit-bourgeois worthies bored by their otherwise humdrum lives. Sean O'Casey, a long-time League member, captured something of the movement's suburban prissiness, describing the 'respectable, white collared, trim suited Gaelic Leaguers' as being 'snug in their selected branches, living rosily in Whitehall, Drumcondra, Rathgar, Donnybrook and all the other nicer habitations of the city'.[1] Clearly these were not men of action.

In addition to this line of attack, it can also be argued that the movement was little more than a form of escapism: a retreat from a world that was modernising at a frightening rate into the misty realms of a Gaelic past that never was. In that sense the revival was perhaps more a symptom than a cause of change. Clearly any movement that allows its leader (Douglas Hyde) to call himself 'The Delightful Little Branch' is open to the charge of being in retreat from reality. And this charge is a serious one. Arguably the movement was profoundly unrealistic. Its great causes, the revival of the language and indeed the reversal of the roles of the languages of English and Irish, look now to have been collective fantasies. The decline of Irish continued apace despite the League.

But this may be a little unfair. At the municipal level the League and its supporters did stage realistic and effective campaigns on behalf of the Irish language. In 1899 Professor Mahaffy of Trinity

College mounted an attack on the teaching of Irish in schools. Hyde waged a campaign against the Trinity man and, once the press began to magnify the debate, the League found itself, for the first time, at the head of a popular campaign. Hyde was eventually successful and Mahaffy backed down. The whole affair gave a huge boost to the fortunes and notoriety of the League, if doing relatively little for the language. At this sort of local level, with such a limited and focused objective the League showed itself able to act politically without difficulty. But step beyond the language question and political opinions flew in all directions.

To get any sort of understanding of the relationship between cultural and political nationalism in this period it is important to recognise that they did not exist in entirely separate arenas. Membership of the Gaelic League, for example, did not preclude membership of the more overtly political groups. Indeed it would appear that all manner of nationalisms, ranging from Fenianism to the scholarly collecting of folk tales, overlapped messily with one another. Patrick Pearse, for example, whilst ostensibly a respectable schoolteacher member of the League, was also an IRB man; and yet oddly, as late as 1912, Patrick Pearse was still talking about his support for Redmond's Home Rule party. In Irish nationalist circles, it seems, all cards were being played simultaneously.

But maybe we can be a little more accurate about the chronological sequencing of events. Though there is some truth in the view that the fall of Parnell triggered a kind of identity crisis in Irish nationalism, hence all the cultural heart-searching for the source of Irishness, it is also true that more traditional forms of political action, both violent and non-violent, revived far more quickly than is often assumed. The first catalyst for this was undoubtedly the Boer War of 1899–1902. The news of a handful of farmers taking on the British Empire inevitably stirred the Irish imagination. Irish brigades formed to support the Boers, though it should be remembered that many more Irishmen were actually fighting against the Boers, given the high numbers of Irish in the British army. Nevertheless, the war created a little excitement back in Dublin and prompted the forming of yet another nationalist group, namely Sinn Féin, under the leadership of Arthur Griffiths. Sinn Féin, like so many groups at this time, borrowed heavily the arguments and dispositions of the League (the choice of a Gaelic name, Sinn Féin, meaning 'Ourselves Alone', for example) but was also more openly political. Griffiths developed what he termed his 'Hungarian' policy, arguing that Ireland must become like Hungary in the

Austro-Hungarian Empire: a joint partner. To this end he advocated that Irish MPs should simply withdraw from Westminster and declare a co-equal Parliament in Dublin. Though this idea would actually be implemented in 1919, at this point, before the Great War, it was regarded as wildly unrealistic, and even so fierce a nationalist as D.P. Moran disparaged Sinn Féin as a 'broad troupe of comedians'.[2]

Even the IPP was not quite so comatose in the early years of the century as it is often portrayed. Redmond worked quietly with the Conservatives to help push through the Wyndham Act of 1903. This Act, through its provisions for state-supported land purchase, led to what might be called a silent revolution in land ownership which did more to transform the social structure of Ireland and diffuse the Land Question than anything that had gone before. Moreover, it must be allowed that Redmond and the IPP seemed more than capable of containing the threat from all the supposedly more energetic nationalist groupings in Ireland. Neither the IRB, nor Sinn Féin, nor the League, nor any other force, came close to Redmond in terms of leadership of Ireland before the war. Redmond should not be seen as a pale imitation of Parnell. In many ways he came much closer to success than Parnell, and his ultimate failure was the result, not of his own shortcomings, but of Asquith's failure of nerve in the face of Loyalist-Tory threats of a civil war.

Evidently, then, traditional politics still remained the principal hope of meaningful change in Ireland up to 1914. Nevertheless it is also true that beneath the surface of Irish nationalism the revivalists had altered the debates and attitudes profoundly. Though this in some ways deepened the ideology of Irish nationalism it can also be seen as introducing some dangerous notes of racial and sectarian hatred.

Despite the fact that Home Rule would dominate Anglo-Irish relations between 1910 and 1914 it would be the rhetoric of cultural nationalism – wedded through small groups of intense young men to the violent traditions of the Fenians – that would prove to be the most influential in the longer run.

Questions

1. In what ways did developments in the cultural sphere affect the growth of Irish nationalism between 1890 and 1910?

2.   Assess Asquith's handling of Irish problems between
      1910 and 1914.

ANALYSIS (2): HOW SUCCESSFUL WAS UNIONISM BETWEEN 1890 AND 1914?

Unionism as a political force grew out of Protestant fears that 'Home
Rule' would mean 'Rome Rule'. But in that basic fact lay the problem
for Unionists. The 1884 Reform Act effectively ushered in the age of
mass politics, with over 60 per cent of adult males having the vote.
Only in certain parts of Ulster, however, were Protestants living in
sufficient number for them to be able to wield any influence at the
ballot box. As a result those Unionists who hoped to maintain all
of Ireland under the Union found themselves in a weak position,
particularly as Parnell's IPP, itself firmly wedded to the idea of
Home Rule, steadily strengthened its electoral grip on the nation.
Gradually it became clear that all-Ireland Unionism as represented
by such rather genteel organisations as the Irish Loyal and Patriotic
Union (ILPU) would not be strong enough to resist Home Rule. As a
result, Unionism became identified with Ulster alone.
    Not only did Gladstone's first attempt at Home Rule in 1886 see
the birth of Unionism as a political movement, it also saw the forging
of a particularly powerful alliance. In February 1886 Lord Randolph
Churchill urged his party, with more than a little dose of opportunism, to 'play the Orange card'. This they duly did and the alliance
between Conservatism and Unionism grew stronger in the years
thereafter, so much so that the Conservative Party began to call
itself the Conservative and Unionist Party.
    Gladstone's two attempts to give Home Rule to Ireland both failed.
In 1886 the bill was defeated in the Commons. In 1893 it was defeated
in the Lords. So strong was the Unionist bias in the Lords that it
seemed to many that there was an in-built constitutional guarantee
against Home Rule ever becoming legislation. As a result of that,
coupled with Gladstone's retirement and the damaging impact of
the Parnell scandal on the IPP, after 1893 Home Rule ceased to be
an issue in British politics.
    Not until the elections of 1910 did Home Rule rear its head again.
The second election of 1910 left the IPP, now under John Redmond,
holding the balance of power between the parties. The Liberals
needed their support but Redmond demanded Home Rule as his
price. To the rage of the Unionist camp, it was a price Asquith

seemed prepared to pay. When Asquith subsequently re
Lords' veto in the 1911 Parliament Act he not only ind
more rage (so much so that the opposition in the Comm
not let Asquith speak, preferring to hurl insults at him fo
an hour), he removed the one serious obstacle to Home
stage was then set for one of the most explosive confrontations in
modern British history.

When Asquith first introduced the third Home Rule bill in 1912,
knowing he had the support not only of the IPP but also of the
Labour Party in the Commons, and given that the Lords could not
now block the bill, the Ulster Unionist position seemed very weak.

But the Ulster cause had an exceptionally able, and fiercely determined, leader. Edward Carson had emerged in 1910 as the leader of
the Irish Unionists in the Commons. In private Carson was a complex
and rather philosophical man but, as A.T.Q. Stewart put it, 'his public
face was set permanently in a scowl of righteous defiance'.[3] He was
known as a particularly ruthless adversary in debate, a reputation he
acquired earlier as an exceptionally fierce Crown prosecutor. As the
struggle unfolded Carson seemed to grow in stature until he came
almost to embody the spirit of godly resistance that characterised
the Ulster movement. His plan was simple: to destroy, or at least
severely modify, the Home Rule bill.

To this end Carson and his able lieutenant James Craig orche-
strated a clever campaign against Asquith's bill. Tactically Carson
played a double game: manoeuvring and negotiating in Parliament
but simultaneously mobilising a mass movement in Ulster.

The defining event in this mobilisation occurred when Carson
and Craig organised the mass signing of the Solemn League and
Covenant, in effect a pledge to resist Home Rule, by over 400,000
people in Belfast on 28 September 1912. Some people signed in
blood and orderly queues of signatories continued to file into the
City Hall long into the night, whilst outside Protestant pipe-and-
drum bands played rousing battle hymns such as 'O God our Help
in Ages Past'.

But in addition to the signing and the rhetoric there was a further
element which was to give Carson's campaign a rather more
menacing edge: the drilling of the young men from the Unionist
clubs with mock rifles and a very serious look in their eyes. It did
not take long before this pretend militarism evolved into the real
thing. In January 1913 the Ulster Volunteer Force (UVF) was
formed, a militia with the aim of resisting by force if necessary,
though whom they would actually fight was not clear, particularly

when many senior officers of the British military made it quite clear that they would not fire upon men so ardently loyal to the Crown. Their feelings were made very clear in the so-called 'Curragh Mutiny' of March 1914 when sixty British cavalry officers resigned their commissions rather than coerce the Ulster Unionists.

On the surface it appears that Carson was genuinely prepared to resort to armed conflict in order to defeat Home Rule. It has been suggested that Carson was merely using the threat of violence as a means to put pressure on Asquith, and there may be a hint of truth in that. But against that we must set Carson's comment to Craig that he was 'not for a mere game of bluff'.[4] Rather stronger evidence of their readiness to use weapons was the determined way in which the Ulstermen acquired them. Despite the utter illegality of such arming, the UVF developed efficient networks for arms importation, a trade that entered into Loyalist legend with the landing of a massive haul at Larne in April 1914, despite rather feeble efforts by the authorities to prevent it. A little belatedly, the more extreme Irish nationalists responded by organising their own militia: the Irish Volunteers. Civil war seemed increasingly likely. A possibility which Carson was quick to exploit and perhaps even exaggerate.

With an apparently apocalyptic situation developing in Ulster, Carson turned his attentions to the political endgame being played out at Westminster. In this pursuit he had one very powerful ally: Andrew Bonar Law, leader of the Conservative Party. It should be remembered that in theory the Conservatives and the Unionists were all one party but in Parliamentary practice they often behaved more like two separate entities. Not only was Bonar Law prepared to maintain the now traditional Conservative policy of defending Ulster against Home Rule, he was prepared, like Carson, to go to any lengths to achieve it, even apparently supporting the idea of armed resistance. Bonar Law believed that when the Liberals promised Home Rule to the IPP they had engaged in what he called a 'corrupt bargain'. There was some justification for this in that Home Rule had not been an issue in the 1910 elections. Thus Bonar Law was able to suggest that the Liberals were once again proposing major constitutional reform but this time without reference to the will of the British people. Defending Ulster could be presented as defending the old order: Ulster became a sort of symbol of everything that had once made Britain great.

There is little doubt that Bonar Law was sincere in his passionate hostility to Asquith's proposals. Although Canadian by birth, he was the son of a Presbyterian minister who had been born in Ulster. Nevertheless it is also true that for many of the less committed in the party ranks, Ulster was seen as a useful means of derailing the Liberals. Carson knew this and exploited these party-political considerations with great skill.

As for the Liberals themselves, there was great uncertainty as to which course to follow. They had shown by their failure to act against the drilling of the UVF that they desperately wished to avoid bloodshed. But in doing this they had perhaps also suggested to Carson that they did not have the stomach to force Home Rule upon Ulster. For a brief while Asquith tried to pretend otherwise. In 1912 he spoke firmly of Ireland as 'one nation and not two', implying one policy for the whole country. But behind the scenes he was panicking at the prospect of civil war. Carson continued to talk as if a bloodbath would be preferable to Home Rule, and eventually Asquith began to weaken. In December 1913, when the Home Rule bill for Ireland had passed its third reading in the Commons and was only a matter of months away from becoming law, he began secret negotiations with Carson.

Carson still harboured hopes of sinking Home Rule altogether but Asquith offered him the idea of a six-year opt-out for the Protestant counties of the north. Once this concession had been placed on the table Carson knew that at least some part of Ulster could be saved. Inevitably he rejected Asquith's deal as nothing more than a stay of execution. The Liberals and the Unionists then entered into several months of proposals and counter-proposals. The king even arranged the Buckingham Palace Conference on the question of Ulster in July 1914, but each and every effort came to nothing. By August 1914 the Ulster Unionists had succeeded in paralysing the whole process to such an extent that when the Great War broke out, it came as almost a relief to Asquith. The Home Rule legislation was suspended for the duration of the war. In reality, Carson had come quite close to his aim of killing Home Rule altogether. But perhaps an even greater achievement, and certainly a pointer for the future, was the fact that he had succeeded in getting the government to recognise, in principle, that at least some part of Ulster should be treated differently from the rest of Ireland. Thus it appears that Carson's greatest achievement was to lay the groundwork for the idea of partition.

Whether this was a triumph or a tragedy is yet more debatable. For moderate nationalists and supporters of Redmond, it was a disaster brought about by Asquith's weakness. Ulster Protestants tend to see it as yet another page of glorious resistance. Oddly enough the key player in this drama, Edward Carson, had great misgivings about his triumph. Carson was from the south and his initial aim had been to maintain all Ireland under the Union. In saving the north he was well aware that he had to some extent undermined the position of the rest of Ireland. More worrying still, though Carson could not have known this at the time, he had established the dangerous principle that the British government only listens when the threat of violence stands behind the rhetoric. Some of the more extreme Irish nationalists, such as Patrick Pearse and the men of Irish Volunteers, were deeply inspired by the armed strategies of the Ulstermen. In that sense Carson and the UVF, despite their political success in defending Ulster, had unwittingly opened a new era in Anglo-Irish relations: an era in which the gun would decide.

Questions

1. Carson and Bonar Law effectively outwitted Redmond and Asquith in the Home Rule crisis of 1912 to 1914. Discuss.
2. Explain why Unionists felt so hostile to Home Rule.

SOURCES

1. DEFINING THE NATION

Source A: Address known as 'The Necessity for De-Anglicising Ireland' given by Douglas Hyde to the National Literary Society in Dublin (25 November 1892).

It is a fact, and we must face it as a fact, that although they adopt English habits and copy England in every way, the great bulk of Irishmen and Irishwomen over the whole world are known to be filled with a dull, and ever-abiding animosity against her and – right or wrong – to grieve when she prospers, and joy when she is hurt . . . I believe it is our Gaelic past which, though the Irish race does not recognise it just at present, is really at the bottom of the Irish heart, and prevents us from becoming citizens of the Empire.

Source B: From the nationalist newspaper *The Leader* by D.P. Moran (27 July 1901).

It has been hinted to us that it is our opinion that no one but a Catholic can be an Irishman. We never said so nor do we think so. We are prepared to be perfectly frank with our sympathisers who think we are 'too Catholic'. We have great admiration and respect for Thomas Davis [Young Irelander], but his 'Tolerance' scheme did not work . . . When we look out on Ireland we see that those who believe, or may be immediately induced to believe, in Ireland as a nation are, as matter of fact, Catholics. When we look back on history we find also, as a matter of fact, that those who stood during the last three hundred years for Ireland as an Irish entity were mainly Catholics, and that those who sought to corrupt them and trample on them were mainly non-Catholics.

Source C: From R.F. Foster's *Modern Ireland 1600–1972* (London: Penguin, 1988).

The [Gaelic] League's objective was specifically to revive the use of the Irish language, and introduce it into the educational curriculum at all levels; it campaigned (often successfully) for bilingual street names and signposts – the sort of issue that did claim the attention of Dublin Corporation. The early membership, especially as preserved in the acerbic memories of Sean O'Casey and James Joyce, was respectable, suburban and bourgeois. It was also tiny. Four years after the Gaelic League's foundation, the minutes cautiously record, 'the secretary was authorised to buy a regular minute book'; growth up to 1899 was commensurately slow. The ensuing boom in membership, and more efficient organisation, owed a great deal to the galvanic effect of the Boer War.

Source D: Speech by the IPP leader John Redmond in Limerick (12 October 1913).

Irish Nationalists can never be assenting parties to the mutilation of the Irish nation; Ireland is a unit. It is true that within the bosom of a nation there is room for diversities in the treatment of government and of administration, but a unit Ireland is and a unit Ireland must remain . . . the two-nation theory is to us an abomination and a blasphemy . . .

Source E: From *A History of Ulster* by J. Bardon (Belfast: Blackstaff Press, 1992).

Yet barely six per cent of Ulster's population could speak Irish and the rate of decline was rapid, hastened by emigration and the tendency for native speakers to regard the language as a badge of poverty and social inferiority.

The Gaelic League did much to restore dignity to the Irish language – denounced by the *Morning Post* as 'kitchen kaffir' and by the *Daily Mail* as a 'barbarous tongue' – but apart from some success in urban districts the organisation was unable to halt the decline.

Source F: From D. Fennell's article 'Against Revisionism' (published in the *Irish Review* 4, 1988).

Every nation in its here and now, the people who make up the nation now, have needs with respect to their national history. They need for their collective well being an image of their national past which sustains and energises them personally, and which bonds them together by making their inherited nation seem a value worth adhering to and working for. The modern Irish nation was provided with such a history by scholars whose aim was, often explicitly, to supply it with such a history in place of the nationally useless and undermining histories or pseudo-histories of Ireland written by Englishmen.

Questions

1. Explain briefly what Hyde meant when he called for the de-Anglicisation of Ireland (Source A). (4 marks)
*2. How far do Sources C and E suggest that the Gaelic League was not particularly influential? (6 marks)
3. Explain why the views of D.P. Moran (Source B) might have been in conflict with the views of his fellow nationalist John Redmond (Source D). (6 marks)
4. What arguments might be put forward against those being advanced in Source F? (7 marks)

Worked answer

*2. On the surface, these sources depict a 'tiny club' of deeply bourgeois gentlemen all of whom were so profoundly cautious and conservative in outlook that they found the purchasing of a minute book almost a daring act. In that light, the League might be thought a harmless hobby for a section of the Catholic middle classes desperately seeking some sort of status. In that sense the League was an attempt to throw off that sense of 'social inferiority' which the English press relentlessly encouraged. If we add to this picture the fact that according to Bardon the Irish language remained in decline, and particularly so in Ulster, despite the League's efforts, it is hard to resist the idea that the Gaelic League was rather a marginal element in the development of the Irish nationalist cause. Indeed it seems highly likely that the role of the League was only retrospectively enlarged in order to justify the Gaelicising policies of the politicians of the Free State after 1921.

However, we must be wary of being too dismissive. The very fact that men like de Valera did have a Gaelicising agenda for the Free State is surely testimony to the persuasiveness of the League. Even small things like the little successes over street names, obviously thrown in as the most damning of faint praise by Professor Foster, were nevertheless a kind of daily call to 'think Irish'. The decline of the language did continue despite the League but this was hardly surprising. English was the language of politics and indeed the language of commerce. The League's real triumph was the restoring of 'dignity' not just to the language but to the whole idea of a Gaelic civilisation. It should also be added, of course, that the figures for numbers of Irish-speaking people (6 per cent) applied only to Ulster. Ulster was not typical. The national figure was around 17 per cent. Furthermore the numbers of people in the League did rise dramatically after the turn of the century.

As to the old caricature that the League was a sort of pompous hobby for self-important bank clerks, it must be remembered that the men who have given us this amusing picture were not themselves terribly reliable. O'Casey and Joyce had innumerable axes to grind and instinctively depicted themselves as men of genius trapped in a world of petty mediocrities.

In conclusion, it must be said that these sources are both useful correctives to the Irish nationalist mythologies which see the League as the grand incubator of the 1916 Rising and then as the nursery for many of the Free State leaders. But, that said, the fact remains that the curious blend of Gaelicism and Catholicism put forward by the League did eventually, albeit posthumously, come to dominate the Free State for half a century or more after the Great War.

SOURCES

2. UNIONISM AND THE THREAT OF CIVIL WAR

Source G: From a speech by the Liberal minister Winston Churchill (October 1911).

We must not attach too much importance to these frothings of Edward Carson. I daresay when the worst comes to the worst, we shall find that civil war evaporates in uncivil words.

Source H: From an address by the Conservative leader, Andrew Bonar Law, to an anti-Home Rule rally at Blenheim Palace (27 July 1912).

If an attempt were made to deprive these men [Ulster Protestants] of their birthright — as part of a corrupt Parliamentary bargain — they would be justified in resisting such an attempt by all means in their power, including force. I can imagine no length of resistance to which Ulster can go in which I would not be prepared to support them.

Source I: From a pamphlet entitled 'The Coming Revolution' by Patrick Pearse (November 1913).

I am glad then, that the North has 'begun' . . . I am glad that the Orangemen have armed, for it is a goodly thing to see arms in Irish hands. I should like to see any and every body of Irish citizens armed. We must accustom ourselves to the thought of arms, the sight of arms, the use of arms. We may make mistakes in the beginning and shoot the wrong people; but bloodshed is a cleansing and sanctifying thing, and the nation which regards it as the final horror has lost its manhood. There are many things more horrible than bloodshed; and slavery is one of them.

Source J: Extracts from the Solemn League and Covenant (September 1912).

Being convinced in our consciences that Home Rule would be disastrous to the material well being of Ulster, as well as of the whole of Ireland, subversive of our civil and religious freedom, destructive of our citizenship, and perilous to the unity of the Empire, we, whose names are underwritten, men of Ulster, loyal subjects of His gracious Majesty King George V, humbly relying on the God whom our fathers in the days of stress and trial confidently trusted, do hereby pledge ourselves in solemn Covenant to stand by one another in defending for ourselves and our children our cherished position of equal citizenship in the United Kingdom and in using all means which may be found necessary to defeat the present conspiracy . . .

Source K: From *The Ulster Crisis* by A.T.Q. Stewart (London: Faber, 1967).

So much has been said and written about Carson that at this distance it is not easy to see him in perspective. He has become part of the Irish legend, and most Irishmen, whether they adore or revile his memory, see him as a symbol of partition – he is either the man who saved Ulster or the man who sabotaged his country's independence. Inevitably he has been misrepresented through popular association with attitudes he in fact mistrusted . . . the world saw an austere fighter who made no concessions, the leader of a Protestant crusade . . . there is evidence that this persona was deliberately cultivated.

Questions

1. Does Source H prove that the Bonar Law supported armed resistance to the government? (3 marks)
2. Use Sources G and K and your own knowledge to discuss whether Carson was bluffing. (5 marks)
*3. Explain why a nationalist like Pearse (Source I) was pleased to see his enemies arming. (8 marks)
4. Explain carefully, using Source J and your own knowledge, the various reasons why so many Ulster Protestants objected to Home Rule. (9 marks)

Worked answer

*3. Pearse is not an easy individual to understand. Although he might come across in this source as verging on the psychopathic, it is important to place these words in the context both of his own developing views and the general mood of the time. Pearse was, as his biographer Ruth Dudley Edwards puts it, an 'inveterate romantic'.[5] And for Pearse there was little more romantic than the idea of taking up arms to bring about some decisive act on behalf of Ireland. Even Irishmen taking up arms to oppose him seemed, to him, a step in the right direction: at least the Irish would be settling their own destiny. A civil war might very well have the effect of jolting the whole situation out of the control of England. The fact that these northern Irish were taking up arms in order to stay British (even if that meant, in theory, fighting the British) is only typical of the strangeness of the unfolding situation in 1912–14. More importantly, he felt that the sight of the north arming might, at long last, stimulate complacent nationalists to do the same. Pearse was out of step with majority Irish opinion at this time, most of which was with Redmond if it was political at all, and there is perhaps an air of desperation about his calls for Irishmen to 'accustom themselves to the thought of arms', suggesting that Dublin at least was very far from the tinder-box of Pearse's dreams.

Alternatively it can be argued that, far from resenting Redmond, Pearse hoped that the arming of the Catholic nationalists in response to the Ulster Unionists might help to keep Asquith loyal to his initial pledge to deliver Home Rule. In that sense perhaps Pearse was simply hoping to play a counter-bluff against Carson. But it seems more likely that neither man was bluffing. Pearse's personality was not constructed to enjoy political games-playing. For good or ill, he had something of the religious fanatic about him. It is no accident that he remarked that it was 'a godly thing' to see the north arming. Like religions, nationalist causes need their martyrs and Pearse was all too well aware of this. In some ways he realised that the arming of the north was a step towards what he called a 'red war' which would undoubtedly provide the required martyrs necessary to lift the cause on to a new, and more noble plane.

That said, it is also necessary to consider the general mood in Europe at this point in history. There was, after all, amongst all sorts of very different groups of young men a growing fascination with the idea of violence – for example, the Futurists, the Italian artistic movement which preached violent destruction of all art galleries. The great rush to join up when war broke out in 1914 is only the most famous example of a general idea around that war helped men to realise their manhood and helped nations to do the same. (Ironically Pearse was disgusted with the number of ordinary Catholic Irishmen rushing to fight for the British Empire but evidently some wars are more sanctifying than others.) Nevertheless, it can be argued that Pearse's inflammatory words are, in some general respects, only the commonplaces of earnest young men all over Europe at this time.

But Pearse was undoubtedly also different from the men of 1914. Pearse wanted to die: to achieve what he called the 'blood sacrifice'.

This notion rests on the deeply romantic, and also revolutionary, belief in the transforming moment or event. Pearse believed, along with many of his generation, that war is the true test of a nation's virility and indeed of its soul. A nation that is frightened to fight for itself is, in spiritual terms, a dying nation. For Pearse, insane as it seems at this distance, the prospect of an Irish civil war was a sign of the true spiritual health of the nation.

6

THE MAKING OF A DIVIDED IRELAND, 1914–22

BACKGROUND NARRATIVE

On 4 August 1914 the British government declared war on Germany. John Redmond, the leader of the Irish Parliamentary Party, agreed to accept the suspension of the Home Rule legislation for the duration of the war and declared his party's total support for the war effort. Carson and the Unionists did the same.

Many Irish nationalists were, however, unhappy with Redmond's unconditional pledge of loyalty. Nationalism as a broad movement gradually began to divide. The IPP under Redmond remained supportive of their leader's line but other organisations, such as the Irish Volunteers, split into loyal and revolutionary factions. It soon became clear that there was a militant strand of nationalism which, following Wolfe Tone's logic about 'England's difficulty', saw this as the time when 'Ireland's opportunity' might be grasped most effectively.

Three closely interrelated groups worked together to plan a rising: the Irish Republican Brotherhood, the militant faction of the Irish Volunteers and the Irish Citizen Army (the latter being a nominally Marxist nationalist group under the leadership of James Connolly).

The rising was planned for Easter 1916 and was to be led by the schoolteacher poet, Patrick Pearse, an intense young man who had become convinced that Ireland needed some sort of blood sacrifice. However, the preparatory stage went badly wrong. A consignment of arms, arriving on board the ship *The Aud*, from Germany, was intercepted by the Royal Navy, and the German crew scuttled the ship, sending 20,000 rifles to the bottom of the Irish Sea.

The leader of the Irish Volunteers, Eoin MacNeill, decided to abort the rising and placed an advertisement in the *Sunday Independent* cancelling 'manoeuvres'. But Pearse and Connolly were determined to go ahead. On Easter Monday 1916 Pearse and Connolly and no more than about 1,000 men seized a number of strategic locations in Dublin, including the General Post Office on the steps of which Pearse declared Ireland's freedom and the birth of the republic.

Over the next six days the British called up reinforcements and began to use artillery to shell the rebel positions. On 29 April the insurgents surrendered and were arrested. The rising had failed. At this point Irish public opinion was largely hostile to Pearse and his followers. Martial law was declared and three days after the surrender the British army executed three of the leading rebels, including Pearse, by firing squad. During the next few days descriptive reports of further executions dominated the headlines. James Connolly, who had been wounded in the fighting, was carried to a chair, tied to it and then shot. It was this almost daily diet of executions over ten days which transformed Irish attitudes towards the rising. Though only fifteen of the rebels were actually executed, and most of the initial seventy-seven death sentences were commuted to prison sentences, the shootings seemed to radicalise mainstream Irish opinion.

The first sign of a changing mood revealed itself in the Roscommon by-election in February 1917. Count George Noble Plunkett, the father of Joseph Mary Plunkett – one of the executed rebels of 1916 – stood as an independent nationalist and defeated Redmond's candidate by a wide margin. Sinn Féin quickly began to adapt its rhetoric to fit the new mood, marking itself out as the only party in Ireland advocating a complete separation from Britain. The growth of Sinn Féin was given an extra boost in April 1918 when the government unwittingly stoked anti-British opinion by threatening to introduce conscription in Ireland. The new reality in Ireland finally declared itself in the General Election after the war in December 1918: Sinn Féin won 73 of the 105 Irish seats and the Irish Parliamentary Party was dramatically reduced to seven. Sinn Féin refused to recognise the British Parliament and announced an Irish Parliament in Dublin, the Dáil Eireann, which they duly attended. The new Parliament declared, once again, the free and independent Republic of Ireland. But for all the bravado in this gesture, the republic still remained little more than the collective fantasy of a group of men who believed themselves to be its first ministers. The British government had not the slightest intention of accepting this new body and was still preparing an amended form of Home Rule.

But the government was simultaneously confronted with something rather more persuasive in the form of a bloody war launched against all representatives of British rule in Ireland, directed by the elusive and charismatic Michael Collins.

The Anglo-Irish War (1919–21) began with a series of murderous attacks on the Royal Irish Constabulary (RIC) but rapidly escalated into a prolonged guerrilla war. Collins restyled the Irish Volunteers into the Irish Republican Army (IRA), and developed a style of warfare which the authorities – even with the support of the notoriously brutal 'Black and Tans' and Auxiliaries – found extremely hard to combat. The IRA carried out unpredictable raids on police barracks and numerous ambushes, using small, mobile bands of men known as flying columns. In addition Collins operated a network of spies and informers so successfully that, for once in Anglo-Irish history, the rebels knew more about British plans than the British did about theirs. Such intelligence enabled Collins to carry out daring acts of ruthlessness like the assassination in November 1920 of thirteen British intelligence agents in the Gresham Hotel in Dublin – in itself only the first act in what was to become known as 'Bloody Sunday'.

But Collins knew that he could not, in the long run, hope to defeat the British Empire by military force. In 1921 the president of the Dáil, Eamon de Valera, accepted the offer of a truce and was invited to London to discuss terms. The talks broke down but eventually de Valera instructed Collins to lead a delegation to London to begin new talks. With extreme reluctance in December 1921 Collins signed the Anglo-Irish Treaty. The treaty gave most of Ireland dominion status, on a par with Canada or Australia – though there was a sort of nominal independence in its being allowed to call itself the Irish Free State – but controversially a border was drawn around six of the more Protestant Ulster counties, giving that part of Ireland a separate status as a self-governing part of Britain. The controversy stemmed from the fact that historically Ulster consisted of nine counties but the treaty carefully deleted the three predominantly Catholic counties, Cavan, Monaghan and Donegal, leaving an 'Ulster' that was safely Protestant.

The treaty was bitterly disliked by most nationalists, but Collins argued that it was the best he could achieve at the time and that the border would only be a temporary measure. The Irish Parliament voted narrowly to accept the treaty by 64 to 57. But this did not resolve the matter and once again the nationalist movement began to tear itself apart. In April 1922 a fratricidal civil war began in Ireland between Collins's pro-treaty forces and the anti-treaty men, led by de Valera. The Free Staters were particularly ruthless, executing seventy-seven dissident Republicans many of whom were 'heroes' of the Anglo-Irish War. Though Collins was to win this battle he was to pay dearly for the victory: he was assassinated in his home county of Cork on 22 August 1922. The border remains in place.

ANALYSIS (1): DISCUSS THE VIEW THAT MICHAEL COLLINS DID MORE TO DIVIDE IRELAND THAN TO UNITE IT.

To those who are sympathetic to the Irish Republican cause, Michael Collins stands as perhaps the greatest figure in the entire pantheon of nationalist heroes. His eminence lies in the fact that, unlike all his predecessors, he fought the British to the brink of defeat. He then negotiated the Anglo-Irish Treaty by which the Irish Free State was born. Though this only conferred dominion status upon twenty-six counties of Ireland and left six counties of Ulster out, it was still, arguably, a major step towards full independence. Thus Collins can be seen as the architect of modern Ireland: the kind of hero around whom a nation can rally. But he can also be seen in rather more negative terms.

It must be remembered, for example, that Collins began the so-called Anglo-Irish War (1919–21) by attacking Irishmen and not Englishmen. Almost all of the early targets in the IRA's war against the RIC were ordinary Irish people. Even Collins's campaign of assassination against the plain-clothed detectives in Dublin, the

G-men, was arguably little more than the serial killing of fellow Irish-men. In June 1919, for example, an unarmed, Irish detective sergeant named Smyth, a man with seven children, was shot in the back only yards from his home.[1] It was also true that in some cases IRA raids led to the deaths of innocent civilians. In the famous deadly attack on the Gresham Hotel – in which a team of elite British agents were shot dead in their beds – a young innocent veterinary officer was also killed 'by mistake'. Evidently Collins and his men were quite pre-pared to kill their fellow countrymen in order to seek the freedom of their country.

Furthermore, it seems that Collins's methods did not have the sup-port of the majority of Irish people: the local elections of 1920 show that Sinn Féin, now clearly linked with the war, was a long way from being dominant. In early 1920 there was still a large number of Irish people who might have been persuaded to oppose Collins and support a governmental solution. But Collins had calculated that the IRA's campaign of terror would engender such reprisals that moderate solutions would be rapidly driven from the board.

His calculation proved to be correct. The British government responded to the early campaigns against the police by sending in large numbers of recruits from mainland Britain, many of whom were brutalised veterans of the Great War. These recruits were officially part of the RIC – the British government was trying to main-tain the appearance that this was still merely a policing problem and not a war. But it was the actions of these 'Black and Tans' and 'Auxiliaries' which not only escalated the conflict into a war but also did most to swing Irish opinion behind the IRA and Sinn Féin. The history of the 'Tans' and the 'Auxies' is a history of beatings, house-burnings, torture and open murder of innocent civilians. Their response, for example, to the Gresham Hotel raid, was to open fire on the crowd at a Gaelic football match at Croke Park, kill-ing one player and many spectators. In political terms, Collins sought an escalation and the British government gave it to him. IRA propa-ganda sheets such as the *Irish Bulletin* could now present the conflict as a plausible war and use every atrocity and crude reprisal to unite the majority behind the war effort.

How far the nation supported the IRA remains a hotly contested subject. It appears that in the agrarian heartlands of Ireland, and in the south and west, support was at its strongest and indeed it was in these very areas that the authority of the Dáil was recognised as against that of the British Parliament. But in some ways the people were caught between two violent forces and their response was often brought about more by intimidation than ideology. Nevertheless, it must be accepted that by 1921, though the IRA might have been unable to win the war militarily, it was winning the battle for hearts and minds.

But if Collins was a successful war leader, it is surely his role in the Anglo-Irish Treaty that has left him most open to criticism. The fact that the treaty precipitated a bitter civil war which in turn led to Collins's own death is more than ample evidence of a ferocious divisiveness. The case against Collins can be made in several ways. From the perspective of men like de Valera, who rejected the treaty, Collins had 'sold out' by accepting terms which not only fell short of the independent republic but also entailed the partitioning of the north.

De Valera also argued that the delegation in London had no right to accept terms before showing them to the rest of the 'government' in Dublin, an argument largely undermined by the fact that the Dáil did eventually vote to accept the treaty.

It has also been argued, in Collins's defence, that de Valera, who had already had some unsuccessful meetings with Lloyd George, deliberately sent Collins instead of going himself because he knew that a free and independent republic was not attainable and that therefore those engaged in the negotiations would be bound to fail. Given what happened to Collins, it becomes possible to see de Valera as playing such an extremely Machiavellian game that he was indirectly responsible for Collins's death. That is probably unfair but it does seem a little odd that the man who saw himself as the political leader of Ireland should have refused to go to the discussions which would decide the fate of his country.

On the substantive point that Collins should not have allowed partition, a number of defences might be made. Firstly, the Unionists, under James Craig, had made their utter intransigence plain, and Lloyd George did not seem willing to take them on, particularly given that his coalition government was highly dependent upon Unionist and Conservative support. These factors made the retention of all of Ulster an almost impossible aim. That said, Lloyd George was prepared to offer a concession on the Ulster question which Collins saw as highly significant. The government promised a Boundary Commission which would allow the peoples of the six counties to decide their fate for themselves. Collins believed that this would leave only four counties outside the new Irish state and that these would come under such economic and political pressure to join the Free State that unity would ultimately be inevitable.

Lloyd George encouraged Collins to think in these terms. Collins undoubtedly placed great faith in the idea of the Boundary Commission; but he did not live long enough to see the Commission come briefly into being in 1924 – only to collapse in disarray in 1925, having made no alterations to the border. Perhaps Collins might be accused of a certain naivety in expecting the Commission to deliver the republic but on the other hand the Free State was better than nothing.

The other major criticism, that Collins failed to deliver independence and left the Free State as nothing more than a dominion, is an equally complex question. Undoubtedly de Valera knew, from his talks and correspondence with Lloyd George, that independence for Ireland was not on the agenda. Lloyd George was not slow to threaten a return to war when de Valera tried to raise this issue. In that sense, in merely agreeing to send a delegation to talk in October 1921, Sinn Féin and the IRA had already accepted the reality that something short of full independence would be the only outcome. De Valera had his own rather vague formula: he proposed that Ireland be linked to the British Empire by what he termed 'External Association'. He hoped that in this choice of words he could establish independence whilst simultaneously pledging loyalty. Not surprisingly the British government rejected it. In the end a curious compromise was worked out in which the Dominion of Ireland would be allowed to call itself the 'Irish Free State': a sort of linguistic sleight of hand which appeased few on either side. Collins argued that dominion status was a large step forward: a stepping-stone towards independence. But, sadly for Collins, dominion status carried within it one small but painful reality: the members of the Dáil would have to swear an oath of loyalty to the British king. This was to prove an extremely divisive point, stimulating the heated rhetoric of betrayal. In retrospect it seems odd that this should have been such a sticking point given that any settlement with Britain would have entailed such a pledge. Indeed it seems clear in retrospect that the republican movement might have been more successful had it offered more loyalty in an effort to buy British movement on the 'six county question'. Unfortunately we shall never know whether Lloyd George would have been prepared, or even able, to bully the north into a unitary dominion. What does seem clear is that large parts of the republican movement preferred complete failure to partial success. Given that mentality, Collins cannot be criticised: *any* eventual treaty, within the parameters of the possible, would have been perceived as a sell-out.

In that sense, Collins cannot be entirely blamed for provoking the civil war. But he had played an important role in militarising political life in Ireland. He had deliberately sought to put the gun into politics; it is not therefore surprising that he found it difficult to remove.

Though he preferred to see himself as a soldier, he was also briefly a politician, being Minister for Home Affairs and Minister for Finance between 1921 and 1922. In this sphere he was to prove equally adept. In 1921 he organised a National Loan, a project which raised over £500,000 from Irish subscribers and from America, which gave the Dáil the vital means to govern. Collins disliked the bureaucratic nature of the work but he was surprisingly good at it. How he would have developed as a politician is best left to the counter-factual specialists, but we do know that he was one of the few politicians of the day to have a vision of a future Irish state. His speeches resounded with ideas as ambitious as 'social justice for all' and as futuristic as using the river Shannon to create electricity.

Overall, Collins is best understood as a revolutionary, a man like Lenin or Trotsky, whose overwhelming energy and will-power brought about great changes though not necessarily positive ones. Like all revolutionaries, he generated both enormous devotion and great hatred. The divisiveness of his impact upon Ireland is indisputable. His methods alienated all manner of groups that might have been more receptive to political persuasion. In consequence a six-county Northern Ireland became a reality, and the Irish Parliamentary Party was destroyed. Furthermore, English Liberals and moderate Irish Protestants gave up on the Irish cause and, of course, the entire republican movement was also split in the process – indeed the main political parties in Ireland today, Fine Gael and Fianna Fáil, owe their origins to the pro- and anti-treaty factions. More subtly it might well be argued that the very idea of Michael Collins has haunted Irish history. He undoubtedly brought a certain glamour to the role of the gunman, a glamour that Irish historians and film-makers have helped to promote. By contrast, the plodding politics of compromise appear feeble. This may, in the final assessment, be the most damaging legacy of all.

Questions

1. Michael Collins was a great military leader but a poor politician. Discuss.

2. Explain why the IRA of 1919–21 was more successful, in military terms, than the rebels of 1916.
3. Between 1916 and 1921 the British government and military handled the problems in Ireland with spectacular incompetence. Discuss.

ANALYSIS (2): WHY WAS IRELAND PARTITIONED?

It might be thought that there is a relatively straightforward answer to this question, namely that Ireland was partitioned along sectarian lines in order to keep its Protestants and Catholics apart, but this would not be entirely true. The six counties of Ulster contained a large number of Catholics, just as the Free State contained a large, but too often overlooked, group of Protestants.

The anomalies created by partition were numerous. Six-county Ulster included the two predominantly Catholic counties of Fermanagh and Tyrone but it also left out such areas as east Donegal which held a large population of Protestants. Many such Unionists felt betrayed, just as many Ulster Catholics felt marooned in a new state. Evidently the precise nature of the partitioning of Ireland was not directed exclusively by sectarian or even ethnic boundaries. In fact, the partitioning of Ireland was in large part the by-product of a very particular constellation of political, economic and military pressures.

To understand why the border followed the route that it did we have to go back, at least, to the Government of Ireland Act of 1920. This particular Act is best thought of as the fourth attempt to pass Home Rule. The Act proposed two Parliaments, one in Dublin and one in Belfast. As we have seen, Sinn Féin had by 1919 already rejected Home Rule and established its own Dáil, but the Unionists accepted the Act, thereby creating an almost laughable situation in which the only part of Ireland to attain Home Rule was the part that had most vehemently opposed it. But this Home Rule was emphatically not 'Rome Rule'; instead it created a Belfast Parliament that could be dominated by Protestants. More to the point, Craig and the Ulster Unionists fought hard during the various stages of the bill to establish a state that would be as large as possible without risking the possibility that the Catholics might reach anything close to 50 per cent. It was for this reason that the Unionists, despite their rhetoric about defending every last Ulsterman, chose to leave the more Catholic counties of Cavan, Monaghan and Donegal to their fate in the South. The 1920 Act thereby redrew the nine-county map of Ulster, creating a six-county state; thus in some ways, the Unionists had virtually settled the border question, to their liking, well before Michael Collins and his delegation came to London to discuss terms in the following year.

But Sinn Féin had also played its part in creating the northern state. In the General Election of 1918 Sinn Féin dramatically replaced the IPP in the electoral hearts of Irish nationalists, winning 73 seats as against the IPP's seven. On the surface, this result should have strengthened the nationalist position – even today it is frequently referred to as the moment when the majority of people in Ireland actually first voted for independence – but, because Sinn Féin then took the decision to boycott Westminster and establish its own Parliament, the effect was to critically weaken the nationalist cause in terms of its influence over political decisions. As a result the Unionists met little opposition in the debates over the treaty. Though the motives of Sinn Féin may have been idealistic by its own lights, the practical effect of its policy was to make the partitioning of Ireland far easier. In that sense Sinn Féin virtually assisted in bringing about the situation that it has spent the subsequent years railing against.

It can be argued, however, that the decision to partition Ireland had effectively been taken before the Great War and that the IPP under Redmond had tacitly accepted it. Certainly it is true that the Home Rule legislation passed in 1914 and suspended by the war contained an opt-out clause for parts of Ulster. But exactly which counties might be left out and for how long was left unclear. Asquith had attempted to persuade the Unionists that they should be excluded from the provisions of the Home Rule Act for a six-year period. Carson rejected this as a mere 'stay of execution'.[2] Nevertheless, the situation in 1914 was sufficiently unclear to allow both Carson and Redmond to hope that the eventual outcome would be acceptable to their respective followers. By 1914 the idea of a separate destiny for Protestant Ulster had entered the debate but was still a long way from being more than an idea.

Events during the war were to force the issue. The Easter Rising, for all its inclusive nationalist rhetoric, was in many ways a very Catholic affair. Pearse deliberately sought a blood sacrifice during Easter week in order to baptise the rising in blood, a gesture which, in some obscure way, resonated with Catholic sensibilities. More measurably, Pearse and his followers in 1916 were steeped in the ideas of the Gaelic League and the Gaelic Athletic Association.

Theirs was a nationalism that stressed the primacy of the language and of the ancient Gaelic culture that was emphatically Catholic and not Protestant. The existence of Connolly's Irish Marxists in Dublin in 1916 may suggest that this event was not quite so ideologically exclusive but Connolly had nowhere near the following of the Gaelicist movements and perhaps the most significant thing about Connolly's involvement in the rising was not his secular outlook but the fact that before he was executed he agreed to receive the last rights from a Catholic priest. In this, and in the gruesome nature of his execution, the atheistic Marxist duly attained his Catholic martyrdom.

Although it is routinely said that the rebels of 1916 gradually acquired posthumous support, this was not the case in north-east Ulster. There the rising only served to widen the rift between the religious communities. Again it is hard to resist the view that in some ways the more extreme rebels of 1916 helped to drive the wedge into the Irish nation whilst simultaneously decrying this development.

The role of the British government in the partitioning of Ireland also requires close attention. Seen from a nationalist perspective, the Liberal and coalition governments appear relatively spineless in the face of Ulster threats. Certainly it is a matter of some surprise that Asquith allowed the Ulster Volunteer Force to drill openly between 1913 and 1914 when their express intent was to use force to defeat the wishes of a legitimately elected government. The fact that the UVF was able to land 25,000 rifles and three million rounds of ammunition at Larne in April 1914, without the slightest hindrance from either the army or the police, does seem to suggest that the authorities on the ground were sympathetic to the Unionist cause. A double standard was exposed more clearly when the Irish volunteers carried out their own gun-running drama only to find the British army opening fire. Three innocent civilians were killed on Bachelor's Walk in Dublin.

But it seems a little crude to see the British government as conspiring on behalf of Unionism. More likely, Asquith was simply floundering after a policy. At best we might say that Asquith chose to tactically ignore the issue in the hope of not inflaming the situation. Instead he merely allowed the contagion of militarism to spread to the nationalist side. The relatively successful episodes of gun-running by both sides is a testament to the government's powers of vacillation. Arguably, therefore, the government had given a clear message, even before 1914, that military force would be allowed to have its say. The partitioning of Ireland would be in large part determined by military factors. In that sense, both six-county Ulster and the Free State were brought about by British weakness in the face of military action or threats of action.

But even allowing for the determining power of the gun from 1914 to 1921, it remains important to focus on the political endgame of 1920 to 1921. It is critical to remember that when Lloyd George sat down to discuss the resolution of the Anglo-Irish War, he was the leader of a coalition government whose future depended upon the continued support of Conservatives under the staunchly Unionist Bonar Law. Despite personally favouring a unitary solution, Lloyd George was not a man to let principles stand in his way. For Lloyd George, political circumstances positively ruled out a united Ireland, a situation of which de Valera must have been aware. This, coupled with the military realities in Ireland, left Collins with very little room for manoeuvre. Lloyd George also used all his dazzling persuasive talents to finesse the Irish delegation into accepting the treaty before contacting de Valera in Dublin.

Although there is some truth in the view that Collins hoped the promised Boundary Commission would destabilise the border and lead to its eventual disappearance, it still seems reasonable to conclude that the Anglo-Irish Treaty, and the border established as a result of it, was not so much a collective and freely agreed decision but a sort of fault-line determined by underlying political and military realities.

Questions

1. Assess Carson's handling of the Unionist cause between 1912 and 1921.
2. Explain why Home Rule provoked such fierce opposition in parts of Ulster.
3. How successful were English governments in dealing with problems in Ireland between 1912 and 1921?

SOURCES

1. THE EASTER RISING, 1916

Source A: A letter from Sir Roger Casement to Eoin MacNeill, written in Berlin, 14 November 1914.

Once our people, clergy and volunteers know that Germany, if victorious, will do her best to aid us in our efforts to achieve an independent Ireland, every man at home must stand for Germany and Irish freedom. I am entirely assured of the goodwill of this Government towards our country, and beg you to proclaim it far and wide. They will do all in their power to help us to win national freedom.

Source B: From Patrick Pearse's speech to the court-martial, 2 May 1916.

We seem to have lost. We have not lost. To refuse to fight would have been to lose; to fight is to win. We have kept faith with the past, and handed on a tradition to the future.

Source C: From the memoirs of the Countess of Fingall (*Seventy Years Young*, Dublin: Lilliput Press, 1991).

General Blackadder, who was President of the Courts-Martial, used to dine with us sometimes. He came to dinner one night greatly depressed. I asked him, 'what is the matter?' He answered: 'I have just done one of the hardest tasks I have ever had to do. I have had to condemn to death one of the finest characters I have ever come across [Pearse]. There must be something very wrong in the state of things that makes a man like that a Rebel. I don't wonder that his pupils adored him.'

Source D: From John Dillon's speech in Parliament (11 May 1916). Dillon was a leading member of Redmond's Irish Parliamentary Party.

The great bulk of the population were not favourable to the insurrection. They got no popular support whatever. What is happening is that thousands of people in Dublin, who ten days ago were bitterly opposed to the whole of the Sinn Féin movement and to the rebellion, are now becoming infuriated against the government on account of these executions, that feeling is spreading throughout the country in a most dangerous degree . . .

Source E: From George Bernard Shaw's letter to the *Daily News* (10 May 1916).

My own view is that men who were shot in cold blood, after their capture or surrender, were prisoners of war, and that it was therefore entirely incorrect to slaughter them. It is absolutely impossible to slaughter a man in this position without making him a martyr and a hero, even though the day before he may have been only a minor poet.

Source F: *Lady Gregory's Journals, 1916–1930* (ed. Lennox Robinson. London: Putnam & Company Ltd, 1946). A recollection of a statement by General Maxwell, the British Military Governor during the period of martial law after the rising.

I am going to punish the offenders, four of them are to be shot tomorrow morning. I am going to ensure that there will be no treason whispered, even whispered, in Ireland for a hundred years.

Questions

1. Explain briefly why Source E argues that it was 'entirely incorrect' to execute the rebels. (4 marks)
*2. How useful is Source A as evidence of Sir Roger Casement's treason? (5 marks)
3. Do Sources C and E support the view that the British authorities reacted brutally against those involved in the rising? (7 marks)
4. Use these sources, and your own knowledge, to discuss the view put forward in Source B. (9 marks)

Worked answer

*2. Source A leaves little doubt about Casement's hopes for the outcome of the Great War. He was actively supporting Germany in the dubious hope that the Kaiser would prove to be a friend to liberty. When he declared that 'every man at home must stand for Germany', it was undoubtedly a clear call for Irishmen to turn against Britain. To urge MacNeill to 'proclaim it' was, in effect, to call for a propaganda campaign in Ireland in favour of Germany. Given that Britain was at war with Germany and drawing many volunteers from Ireland,

Casement's comments surely cannot be construed as anything other than extreme disloyalty to the sovereign, which is the definition of treason. In addition to that, it is evident from the source that Casement was not indulging in mere rhetoric: he was writing from Berlin and had clearly been in some sort of negotiation with German intelligence. In fact, as we know, he was also in the process of obtaining the weaponry necessary for the planned rising. A less well-known fact is that he was also urging Germany to release Irish prisoners of war from the British side in order to create an 'Irish Brigade' which would then, according to Casement at least, happily fight for Germany. These bits of background information, taken in conjunction with his own words, leave little room for doubt about the verdict which led to his eventual hanging.

Nevertheless, various counter-arguments can be put forward. Casement argued that, as an Irishman, he did not recognise the authority of the British sovereign and could not therefore be accused of disloyalty. This argument was fatally undermined by the fact that Casement had accepted a knighthood from the Crown only five years before.

It might be objected that what the source reveals is not so much treason as foolishness. Casement blithely accepts the 'goodwill' of Germany and sees no apparent difficulty in the idea that Irish opinion, both in Ireland and in German POW camps, might easily be thrown into reverse. It might be argued, therefore, that the source could be used to show just how far Casement had entered the realms of fantasy. But again events undermine the argument: Germany *did* send arms and if they had not been intercepted the rising might have impacted much more effectively on the general British war effort.

Lastly, it has been argued that the fact that the chief prosecutor in Casement's trial was F.E. Smith – a Tory Unionist who had been actively involved in Ulster gun-running before the war – should invalidate the case. There may be a serious procedural point here but it is surely not one which in any way detracts from Casement's guilt. Perhaps the only argument which might have saved Casement would have been the same one that saved the majority of rebels from the death sentence: namely that it was tactically better for the British to at least appear to be magnanimous. But most of the other rebels had not left such explicit letters; and none of the other rebels had recently accepted knighthoods. In the end it seems that Casement was not attempting to conceal his aims: the letter is not just proof of treason; it is part of an open and enthusiastic embracing of it.

SOURCES

2. THE ANGLO-IRISH WAR 1919–21

Source G: From W.B. Yeats's poem 'Sixteen Dead Men', published during the Anglo-Irish war. (Reprinted by permission of A.P. Watt Ltd on behalf of Michael B. Yeats.)

> O but we talked at large before
> The sixteen men were shot,
> But who can talk of give and take
> What should be and what not
> While those dead men are loitering there
> To stir the boiling pot?

Source H: A description of Collins addressing a meeting of Sinn Féin in February 1919.

He spoke with much more vehemence and emphasis, saying that the sooner fighting was forced and a general state of disorder created throughout the country the better it would be for the country. Ireland was likely to get more out of the state of general disorder than from a continuance of the situation as it then stood.

Source I: From an address by a Black and Tan commander, Lt. Col. Smyth, to his men, 17 June 1920. (A constable with Sinn Féin sympathies later reported these words to the nationalist *Irish Bulletin*.)

If a police barracks is burned or if the barracks already occupied is not suitable, then the best house in the locality is to be commandeered, the occupants thrown out into the gutter. Let them die there, the more the merrier . . . the more you shoot, the better I will like you, and I assure you no policeman will get into trouble for shooting anyone.[3]

Source J: From a speech by Edward Carson in the House of Lords (December 1921).

If you tell your Empire in India, in Egypt and all over the world that you have not got the men, the money, the pluck, the inclination and the backing to restore order in a country within twenty miles of your own shore, you may as well begin to abandon the attempt to make British rule prevail throughout the Empire at all.

Source K: From Lloyd George's letter to de Valera attempting to set out the terms upon which Britain was prepared to negotiate (August 1921).

We must direct your attention to one point upon which you lay some emphasis, and upon which no British Government can compromise, namely, the claim that we should acknowledge the right of Ireland to secede from her allegiance to the King. No such right can ever be acknowledged by us. The geographical propinquity of Ireland to the British Isles is a fundamental fact. The history of the two islands, however it is read, is sufficient proof that their destinies are indissolubly linked.

Questions

*1. Explain what Yeats meant by 'to stir the boiling pot' in Source G. (4 marks)
2. Explain how the arguments put forward against the nationalist cause in Sources J and K differ in their reasoning. (6 marks)
3. How reliable is Source I as evidence of Black and Tan brutality? (6 marks)
4. Use these sources and your own knowledge to discuss the view that the Anglo-Irish Treaty was the product of a combination of bravado on the part of the nationalists and weakness on the part of the British government. (9 marks)

Worked answer

*1. To decode metaphor is always a difficult and delicate task and one which runs the risk of vulgarising the meanings of the poet. Having said that, it seems reasonable to infer that Yeats saw the Ireland of the Anglo-Irish War as the 'boiling pot': a vortex of violent forces moving towards some sort of climax. The 'Sixteen Dead Men' of the Easter Rising had stirred Ireland in the manner of their deaths (the fact that Roger Casement was hanged and not shot is, in poetic terms, irrelevant) and in so doing inspired Collins and the IRA.

More subtly, perhaps, Yeats is referring to the collective pool of nationalist memory and mythology. The Irish nationalist movement from Wolfe Tone to Pearse had nourished itself on its martyrs, paradoxically drawing strength from each defeat. In that sense Yeats is playing with the inverted Irish logic in which defeat is also victory and dead men are more powerful than those 'at large'. In so doing of course, despite the ambiguous tone of the poem and its regret about the death of 'give and take', Yeats, the nationalist, was also doing his own bit of stirring.

NOTES

INTRODUCTION

1 Frank Pakenham (Lord Longford), *Peace by Ordeal* (London: Pimlico, 1972, first published 1935), p. 74.

1. REVOLUTIONS AND REACTIONS, 1775–1800

1 Sir Charles Ross (ed.), The *Cornwallis Correspondence* (London: Murray, 1859), vol. 3, p. 102.
2 Ibid., p. 103.

2. THE AGE OF THE LIBERATOR, 1800–45

1 O. MacDonagh, *The Life of Daniel O'Connell* (London: Allen Lane, 1991), p. 187.

3. THE GREAT FAMINE AND ITS LEGACY, 1845–70

1 John Mitchel, quoted in Cormac Ó Gráda, *The Great Irish Famine* (London: Macmillan, 1989), p. 11.
2 L.P. Curtis, Jr, *Anglo-Saxons and Celts: A Study of Anti-Irish Prejudice in Victorian England* (Bridgeport, Conn.: Conference on British Studies, 1968), p. 50.
3 Ibid., p. 52.
4 Charles Edward Trevelyan, quoted in Colm Tóibín, *The Irish Famine* (London: Profile, 1999), p. 40.

5 Cormac Ó Gráda, *The Great Irish Famine* (London: Macmillan, 1989), p. 76.

6 Manna: a biblical reference to food miraculously provided. Salient waters are waters literally leaping with fish.

4. THE AGE OF PARNELL, 1870–90

1 Michael Davitt, quoted in M.J. Winstanley, *Ireland and the Land Question 1800–1922* (London: Methuen, 1984), p. 18.

2 John Devoy, telegram to Parnell, reported in the *New York Herald*, 26 October 1878, quoted in A.C. Hepburn, *The Conflict of Nationality in Modern Ireland* (London: Edward Arnold, 1980), p. 41.

3 Lord Randolph Churchill, letter to James Fitzgibbon, 16 February 1886, quoted in W.S. Churchill, *Lord Randolph Churchill* (London: Macmillan, 1906), vol. 2, p. 59.

4 Charles Stewart Parnell, Galway by-election address, 10 February 1886, quoted in C. O'Clery (ed.), *Phrases Make History Here* (Dublin: O'Brien Press, 1986), p. 25.

5 A.B. Cooke and J.R. Vincent, *The Governing Passion* (Brighton: Hassocks, 1974), p. 18.

6 F.S.L. Lyons, *Charles Stewart Parnell* (London: Fontana, 1991, first published 1977), p. 298.

7 Parnell and Katharine O'Shea were not actually husband and wife. She was still married to Captain O'Shea. Nevertheless, Parnell and Mrs O'Shea were living together and she was carrying their child.

5. CULTURAL NATIONALISM AND UNIONISM, 1890–1914

1 Sean O'Casey, quoted in R. Dudley Edwards, *Patrick Pearse: The Triumph of Failure* (Dublin: Poolbeg Press, 1990, first published 1977), p. 21.

2 D.P. Moran, quoted in R. Kee, *The Green Flag* (London: Penguin, 1989, first published 1972), vol. 2, p. 157.

3 A.T.Q. Stewart, *The Ulster Crisis* (Dublin: Blackstaff Press, 1997, first published 1967), p. 39.

4 Ibid., p. 47.

5 R. Dudley Edwards, *Patrick Pearse: The Triumph of Failure* (Dublin: Poolbeg Press, 1990, first published 1977), p. 38.

6. THE MAKING OF A DIVIDED IRELAND, 1914–22

1 R. Kee, *The Green Flag* (London: Penguin, 1989, first published 1972), vol. 3, p. 81.
2 Edward Carson, speech in Parliament, 9 March 1914, quoted in C. O'Clery, *Phrases Make History Here* (Dublin: O'Brien Press, 1986), p. 44.
3 Lt. Col. Smyth's men refused to follow his orders. He was shot dead one month later in the County Club of Cork by an IRA volunteer.

SELECT BIBLIOGRAPHY

GENERAL BOOKS

The following books cover the entire period in varying degrees of complexity. Robert Kee's three-volume history of Ireland, *The Green Flag* (Harmondsworth: Penguin, 1989), is probably still the most accessible source of basic facts. A more recent general history of Ireland is James Lydon's *The Making of Ireland* (London and New York: Routledge, 1998). A more analytical approach is offered in K. Theodore Hoppen's *Ireland since 1800* (2nd edn, London and New York: Longman, 2001). For those looking for ideas rather than solid surveys, Patrick O'Farrell's *England and Ireland since 1800* (London and New York: Oxford University Press, 1975) is very stimulating, as is O. MacDonagh's *States of Mind: A Study of Anglo-Irish Conflict, 1780–1980* (London and Boston: Allen & Unwin, 1983). For a counter-intuitive approach to the economic ties between England and Ireland, L.M. Cullen's *An Economic History of Ireland since 1660* (London: Batsford, 1972) remains one of the foundation stones of the revisionist school of thought. For students looking for one history which combines the factual with the analytical and also illuminates the historiographical debates behind so much of the narrative, see R.F. Foster's *Modern Ireland* (London: Penguin, 1988). For those interested in the debates surrounding 'revisionism', *Interpreting Irish History: The Debate on Historical Revisionism, 1938–1994* (Blackrock: Irish Academic Press, 1994), edited by Ciaran Brady, contains a number of stimulating articles. An indispensable reference book for the serious student is *The Oxford Companion to Irish History*, edited by S.J. Connolly (Oxford: Oxford University Press, 1998).

COLLECTIONS OF PRIMARY SOURCES

There are relatively few published collections of primary material but the following are useful: A.C. Hepburn, *The Conflict of Nationality in Modern Ireland* (London: E. Arnold, 1980). This offers a wide range of short extracts from key sources. A. Mitchell and P. Ó Snódaigh's *Irish Political Documents 1916–49* (Blackrock: Irish Academic Press, 1985) is obviously limited to the later period. *Irish Historical Documents, 1172–1922*, edited by E. Curtis and R. McDowell (London: Methuen & Co., 1943), is rather antiquated now but still useful. For Unionism, P. Buckland's *Irish Unionism* (Dublin: Gill & Macmillan, 1973) is extremely helpful. The period from 1886 to 1986 is entertainingly covered in *Phrases Make History Here: A Century of Irish Political Quotations, 1886–1986* (Dublin: O'Brien Press, 1986), edited by C. O'Clery.

1 REVOLUTIONS AND REACTIONS, 1775–1800

For a concise study of this period and beyond, *Ireland before the Famine* (Dublin: Gill & Macmillan, 1972) by G. Ó Tuathaigh is still hard to beat. The revolutionary events of 1798 are covered in T. Pakenham's *The Year of Liberty* (London: Hodder & Stoughton, 1969). For a sharp focus on Wolfe Tone, M. Elliott's biography, *Wolfe Tone: Prophet of Irish Independence* (New Haven, Conn.: Yale University Press, 1989), is definitive and her *Partners in Revolution: The United Irishmen and France* (New Haven, Conn.: Yale University Press, 1982) is essential reading for anyone interested in the wider movement. For those with access to a university library, an important primary source is undoubtedly *The Autobiography of Theobald Wolfe Tone, 1763–1798*, edited by R. Barry O'Brien (London: T. Fisher Unwin, 1893). Events in Ulster are well covered in J. Bardon's *A History of Ulster* (Belfast: Blackstaff, 1992) and this book is also useful as a guide to the Ulster dimension throughout the entire period up to 1922. The background to the Act of Union is best covered in *The Passing of the Irish Act of Union: A Study in Parliamentary Politics* by G.C. Bolton (London: Oxford University Press, 1966). For the consequences of the Act, see *Ireland under the Union: Varieties of Tension: Essays in Honour of T.W. Moody*, edited by F.S.L. Lyons and R.A.J. Hawkins (Oxford: Clarendon Press, 1980).

2 THE AGE OF THE LIBERATOR, 1800–45

For Daniel O'Connell the definitive biography is by Oliver Mac-
Donagh, *The Life of Daniel O'Connell, 1775–1887* (London: Weidenfeld
& Nicolson, 1991). For those interested in the English side, Norman
Gash's biography, *Sir Robert Peel: The Life of Sir Robert Peel after
1830* (London: Longman, 1972), makes an interesting contrast. For
the wider political and religious picture, D. Kerr's *Peel, Priests, and
Politics: Sir Robert Peel's Administration and the Roman Catholic
Church in Ireland, 1841–1846* (Oxford: Clarendon Press, 1982) is per-
haps the most authoritative account, although *Catholic Emancipa-
tion: Daniel O'Connell and the Birth of Irish Democracy, 1820–30*
(Dublin: Gill & Macmillan, 1985) by F. O'Ferrall is also very thorough.
For anyone wishing to go further, it should be pointed out that *The
Correspondence of Daniel O'Connell* (Dublin: Irish Manuscripts
Commission, 1972–80) has been published in eight volumes! For
'Young Ireland' see R. Davis's *The Young Ireland Movement*
(Dublin: Gill & Macmillan, 1987). There are interesting discussions
of the different varieties of nationalism in Ireland during this
period in T. Garvin, *The Evolution of Irish Nationalist Politics*
(Dublin: Gill & Macmillan, 1981), and D.G. Boyce's *Nationalism in
Ireland* (London: Croom Helm, 1982).

3 THE GREAT FAMINE AND ITS LEGACY, 1845–70

The classic secondary work on the famine is undoubtedly Cecil
Woodham-Smith's *The Great Hunger* (London: Hamish Hamilton,
1962, now in Penguin). However, this book is now rather old and
blissfully unaware of revisionist history. For a more analytical
approach, see Mary Daly's *The Famine In Ireland* (Dundalk: Dun-
dalgan, 1986) or *The Great Irish Famine* (London: Macmillan, 1989)
by Cormac Ó Gráda. For a stimulating discussion of the wider signi-
ficances of the famine, see Colm Tóibín's *The Irish Famine* (London:
Profile, 1999). For those seeking a clear and concise introduction to
the Land Question in general, M.J. Winstanley's *Ireland and the
Land Question* (London: Methuen, 1984) is extremely helpful. For a
more complex analysis see W.E. Vaughan's *Landlords and Tenants
in Mid-Victorian Ireland* (Oxford: Clarendon Press, 1994). The
economic and social impact of the famine is skilfully delineated in
Ó Gráda's *Ireland: A New Economic History* (Oxford: Clarendon
Press, 1995). For a closer look at attitudes see F. Neal's *Black 47:*

Britain and the Irish Famine (London: Macmillan, 1997.) For those interested in racist attitudes generally, see L.P. Curtis, *Anglo-Saxons and Celts: A Study of Anti-Irish Prejudice in Victorian England* (Bridgeport, Conn.: Conference on British Studies at the University of Bridgeport, 1968).

4 THE AGE OF PARNELL, 1870-90

F.S.L. Lyons's masterful biography, *Charles Stewart Parnell* (London: Collins, 1977), is still the best source of factual information on the Irish leader. Conor Cruise O'Brien's *Parnell and his Party* (Oxford: Clarendon Press, 1957) is a classic and indispensable to anyone seeking to understand Parnell's political machine. See also *C.S. Parnell* (Dublin: Gill & Macmillan, 1980) by P. Bew. An excellent collection of essays on various aspects of the Parnell phenomenon is published as *Parnell in Perspective* (London and New York: Routledge, 1991), edited by D.G. Boyce and A. O'Day. For an intriguing primary source on the Land League see *The Tale of a Great Sham* (written in 1907 but only published by Arlen House in 1986) by Parnell's sister Anna. For those seeking a clear, balanced and relatively short guide to the struggles over Home Rule, see *Home Rule and the Irish Question* (London: Longman, 1980) by G. Morton. The literature on Gladstone is dauntingly extensive but two books stand out as classics: J.L. Hammond's *Gladstone and the Irish Nation* (London: Longman, 1938), which is rather sympathetic to Gladstone, and *The Governing Passion* (Brighton: Harvester Press, 1974) by J.R. Vincent and A.B. Cooke, which attempts to detonate the idea of Gladstone's mission. Although there are biographies of all the protagonists in the Home Rule crisis, a more analytical approach is offered in W.C. Lubenow, *Parliamentary Politics and the Home Rule Crisis* (Oxford: Clarendon Press, 1988), and J. Loughlin, *Gladstone, Home Rule and the Ulster Question* (Dublin: Gill & Macmillan, 1986).

5 CULTURAL NATIONALISM AND UNIONISM, 1890-1914

A primary source of great importance is 'The Necessity of De-Anglicizing Ireland' by Douglas Hyde, in *The Revival of Irish Literature: Addresses by Sir Charles Gavan Duffy, Dr. George Sigerson and Dr. Douglas Hyde* (London, 1894). Of secondary sources on cultural nationalism, see F.S.L. Lyons, *Culture and Anarchy in Ireland 1890–1939* (Oxford: Clarendon Press, 1979). For the Gaelic League see *The Dynamics of Cultural Nationalism* (Hemel Hempstead: Allen & Unwin, 1987) by J. Hutchinson. See also *The Politics of Irish Literature from Thomas Davis to W.B. Yeats* (London: George Allen & Unwin, 1972) by M. Brown. For the pre-war Home Rule crisis see P. Jalland, *The Liberals and Ireland: The Ulster Question in British Politics to 1914* (Brighton: Harvester Press, 1980), and also A.T.Q. Stewart's *The Ulster Crisis* (London: Faber, 1967). A very useful and balanced guide to Anglo-Irish political relations during this period and beyond is provided by D.G. Boyce's *The Irish Question and British Politics 1868–1996* (Basingstoke: Macmillan Education, 1988). Paul Bew's *John Redmond* (Dundalk: Historical Association of Ireland, 1996) fills an important gap in the historiography and might well be read in conjunction with Roy Jenkins's classic biography, *Asquith* (London: Collins, 1964). For an entertaining read, which is amusingly slanted against the British establishment, see George Dangerfield's masterpiece *The Strange Death of Liberal England* (originally published in 1935, now available in an edition from Stanford University Press, 1997).

6   THE MAKING OF A DIVIDED IRELAND, 1914–22

The Easter Rising is best covered in Charles Townshend's *Political Violence in Ireland* (Oxford: Clarendon Press, 1983), although Joseph Lee's textbook, *Ireland 1912–1985* (Cambridge: Cambridge University Press, 1989), is also very useful. Both books adopt a rather iconoclastic approach. For a more reverential source see *The Rising* by D. Ryan (Dublin, 1949) which contains numerous first-hand accounts. There is also an excellent biography of Patrick Pearse appropriately subtitled *The Triumph of Failure* (London: Gollancz, 1977) by R. Dudley Edwards. There also some useful essays in *The Revolution in Ireland 1879–1923,* edited by D.G. Boyce (Basingstoke: Macmillan Education, 1988), including one by C. Townshend on British policy towards Ireland. See also Boyce's *English Men and Irish Troubles: British Public Opinion and the Making of Irish Policy* (London: Cape, 1972). For primary sources on this period see *The Irish Uprising 1914–1921* (London: The Stationery Office, 2000), edited by T. Coates. For the background to the treaty see *The Birth of the Irish Free State 1921–3* (Tuscaloosa, Ala.: University of Alabama Press, 1980) by J.M. Curran. The classic account of the negotiations which created the treaty is undoubtedly *Peace By Ordeal* (first published 1935, fifth edition London: Pimlico, 1992) by Frank Pakenham (Lord Longford) but it is very old and has been criticised for its rather innocent approach to de Valera. For the Ulster angle the best single work is P. Buckland's *Ulster Unionism and the Origins of Northern Ireland* (Dublin, 1973). For a readable narrative of Collins's life see *Michael Collins* by T.P. Coogan (London: Hutchinson, 1990).

INDEX

Collins, Michael 82, 107; and
   Anglo-Irish war 100–1;
   assessment of achievements
   101–5; his desire for disorder
   113; influence of Easter
   Rising on 114; role in treaty
   negotiations 109
Connolly, James 81, 98–9, 108
Conservative Party 29, 30–4,
   66–72, 78, 86, 88, 103
Constructive Unionism 34, 66
Corn Laws 33, 42
Cornwallis, Lord 12, 19
Craig, James 87–8, 103
Cromwell, Oliver 3, 40
Curragh Mutiny 88

Dáil Eireann 100, 102, 106
Davis, Thomas 26, 91
Davitt, Michael 63–4, 66–7, 73
Defender movement 9–10
Destitute Poor (Ireland) Act
   (1847) 43
Devonshire Commission (1843)
   32
devotional revolution 52
Devoy, John 64
Dillon, John 110
Disraeli, Benjamin 46
Dissenters 3–4, 26, 32
Duffy, Charles Gavan 26

Easter Rising 19, 82, 98–9, 107,
   110
Education Act (1831) 24, 28
Enlightenment, the 9, 20–1

Famine, Great 25, 34; British
   attitudes toward 44–8; cause
   and effect of 41–3, 55–6;
   contemporary views 53–4; and
   Corn Law issue 42;

historiography of 47–8, 56–8;
   impact on demography and
   patterns of land ownership
   49–50; nationalist view of 44;
   influence on peasant culture
   and devotional revolution 52;
   Peel's response to 41–2, 45;
   and Poor Law Extension Act
   (1847) 43, 46–7; and potato
   prices 42; Russell's policy
   towards 42–3; and role of
   Trevelyan 44–6, 53–5; Young
   Ireland rebellion during 51
Fenians 1, 20, 37, 67; aims and
   activities 59–60; Gaelic
   Athletic Association and 80;
   and the Great Famine 50, 52;
   legacy 85; Manchester raid 72
Fianna Fáil 105
Fine Gael 105
Fitzgerald, Vesey 23, 35
Foster, John 12–14
free trade 5
French Revolution 5–6, 12,
   16–17, 21
Froude, James 1, 46
Futurist movement 96

Gaelic Athletic Association
   79–80, 82, 107
Gaelic League 80, 82, 91–3, 107
George III, king 13, 19, 22
Germany 98, 110, 111
Gladstone, William:
   achievements of Irish policies
   71–2; alleged mission 60;
   Home Rule and 62–3, 75–8, 86;
   and Land Acts (1870 and
   1881) 51, 60–1, 65–8; attitude
   to Parnell 61; influence of
   Peel on 33; and Phoenix Park
   murders 62, 66; relations with